Party

Fare

Party

Fare

A HEALTHY EXCHANGES® COOKBOOK

JoAnna M. Lund

HELPing Others HELP Themselves
the **Healthy Exchanges**® Way™

A Perigee Book

A Perigee Book
Published by The Berkley Publishing Group
200 Madison Avenue
New York, NY 10016

Copyright © 1997 by Healthy Exchanges, Inc.
Diabetic Exchanges calculated by Rose Hoenig, R.D., L.D.
Book design by Jill Dinneen
Cover design and illustration by Charles Bjorklund
Front-cover photograph of the author by Glamour Shots® of West Des Moines

For more information about Healthy Exchanges products, contact:
Healthy Exchanges, Inc.
P.O. Box 124
DeWitt, Iowa 52742-0124
(319) 659-8234

Perigee Special Sales edition: January 1997
ISBN: 0-399-52325-1
Published simultaneously in Canada.

The Putnam Berkley World Wide Web site address is
http://www.berkley.com/berkley

Printed in the United States of America

10 9 8 7 6 5 4 3 2 1

Before using the recipes and advice in this book, consult your physician or health-care provider to be sure they are appropriate for you. The information in this book is not intended to take the place of any medical advice. It reflects the author's experiences, studies, research, and opinions regarding a healthy lifestyle. All material included in this publication is believed to be accurate. The publisher assumes no responsibility for any health, welfare, or subsequent damage that might be incurred from use of these materials.

This cookbook is dedicated to everyone at QVC, from the on-air hosts to the book buyers, from the production staff to the hardworking order representatives answering the phones. We all have a good time, and we still get the job done. Isn't that a good beginning for a party? (And I've got just the "common folk" healthy recipes for every celebration!)

Contents

Acknowledgments ix

Enjoying the Party Without Fearing the Food 1

Six Tips to Make Buffet Parties Fun 3

JoAnna M. Lund and the Creation of Healthy Exchanges 5

Healthy Exchanges® Weight Loss Choices™/Exchanges 9

Sodium, Fat, Cholesterol, and Processed Foods 17

JoAnna's Ten Commandments of Successful Cooking 22

My Best Healthy Exchanges Tips and Tidbits 25

A Peek Into My Pantry and My Favorite Brands 39

Shopping the Healthy Exchanges Way 42

The Healthy Exchanges Kitchen 48

How to Read a Healthy Exchanges Recipe 51

A Few Cooking Terms to Ease the Way 53

The Recipes

 Party Starters 56

 Sensational Sides 78

 The Main Event 110

 Glorious Endings 148

Index of Recipes 185

Acknowledgments

Anyone who thinks that writing and testing three cookbooks in three months is a "piece of cake"—no matter how easy to prepare the recipes are—needs to think again! It took a lot of teamwork to get this project completed on time. For being members of the Healthy Exchanges Team, I want to thank:

John Duff and Barbara O'Shea from Putnam and Amy Rosen and Paula Piercy from QVC, for cooking up the idea in the first place.

Angela Miller and Coleen O'Shea, for assuring me I could do it.

Shirley Morrow for typing, retyping, and typing again as I changed my mind on what I wanted to include.

Rita Ahlers and Gerry Stamp, for helping me test the recipes.

Janis Jackson and Susan Williams, for doing all those dishes, and I do mean *dishes*, when well over three hundred recipes had to be tested.

Lori Hansen, for lending a hand with the Food Processor II software so the recipes could be as accurate as possible in calories and grams.

Rose Hoenig, R.D., L.D., for calculating the Diabetic Exchanges.

Barbara Alpert, for helping me get my manuscript "ready for the presses" more quickly than I could have alone.

Cliff Lund, my "Official Taste Tester." His taste buds are the "Barometer of America." If he loves it, you can bet your family, your friends, and your neighbors will love it too! And he really loves the recipes in this collection of cookbooks.

The entire Healthy Exchanges crew for giving Cliff a hand with the taste-testing responsibilities.

God, for giving me the ability to create "common folk" healthy recipes. It truly is miraculous what happens when we change our prayers from what we want to what we need.

Party

Fare

Enjoying the Party Without Fearing the Food

For most people, a party invitation promises a chance to visit with friends, celebrate an occasion, and savor lots of good-tasting food. But for anyone who's struggled to lose weight, follow a medically advised food plan, or recover from a health problem, thoughts of a party may be shadowed by concern about what you'll eat, how much you'll eat, and whether what you eat will be good for you!

I used to feel that way lots of times, until I learned how to party in The Healthy Exchanges Way. By taking a positive approach and reminding myself that a party doesn't mean an excuse to binge, I chose to enjoy myself *and* enjoy moderate portions of foods I really liked. But more than that, I decided to create delicious and easy-to-prepare versions of party food that everyone can enjoy.

In this one volume I've collected some of my best-loved and best-tasting special-occasion dishes. As with all Healthy Exchanges recipes, they're low in fat and sugar, they're made from everyday ingredients you can find in any small-town grocery, and they stir up so fast and good you'll be just as delighted as your guests!

Of course, even if every dish on the buffet is prepared in a healthy way, that still doesn't mean you can fill your plate again and again, until you're full to bursting! Even if you're offered an "all-you-can-eat" buffet at a party or restaurant, *you* have to choose what foods will please your palate—and satisfy your soul. But once you've decided on the dishes that bring back wonderful memories or tease your senses, you're free to enjoy them fully!

I think you'll discover, as I have, that life is a series of choices, an "all-you-choose-to-eat" buffet. By selecting your favorites in moderation, but no longer denying yourself real pleasure at parties, you'll enjoy a lifetime of healthy living that tastes as good as it feels!

Jo Anna

Six Tips to Make Buffet Parties Fun (And Easier for the Hostess!)

1. Buffet-style parties involve fewer last-minute hassles than traditional sit-down parties. They also make it easier for guests to pick and choose what they really want to eat. And, because you don't have to worry about having enough space at the table, you can invite more guests. But before you send out the invitations, decide how many people your home can realistically hold, and estimate what it will cost in time and money to offer a generous and varied menu. (It's easy to get carried away!)

2. Arrange the serving table so that the flatware, napkins, and beverages are at the end of the line, so that your guests won't have to balance all of that in their hands while trying to fill their plates.

3. If you have the room, a two-sided buffet works better for large parties. Just be sure to have identical items on both sides so that no one needs to reach across the table. Arrange large platters so they can be reached by people on both sides of the table, and provide serving utensils (resting on decorative plates) on each side.

4. If your guests will be balancing their plates on their laps or standing while eating, try not to serve foods that require cutting. Be sure both the plates and napkins are extra-large and sturdy. This will help to guard against spills on their clothing and your rugs.

5. To make life easier on you, plan your menu around foods that don't need to be kept constantly chilled or piping hot. This will also reduce the risk of your guests suffering from food-related illnesses after the party.

6. Choose decorations and background music that complement your food selections. It's the little things in both food preparation and party planning that make the difference between a party that's just "all right" and a Great Party!

JoAnna M. Lund and the Creation of Healthy Exchanges

For twenty-eight years I was the diet queen of DeWitt, Iowa. I tried every diet I ever heard of, every one I could afford, and every one that found its way to my small town in eastern Iowa. I was willing to try anything that promised to "melt off the pounds," determined to deprive my body in every possible way in order to become thin at last.

I sent away for expensive "miracle" diet pills. I starved myself on the Cambridge Diet and the Bahama Diet. I gobbled Ayds diet candies, took thyroid pills, fiber pills, prescription and over-the-counter diet pills. I went to endless weight-loss support group meetings—but I managed to turn healthy programs such as Overeaters Anonymous, Weight Watchers, and TOPS into unhealthy diets . . . diets I could never follow for more than a few months.

I was determined to discover something that worked long-term, but each new failure increased my desperation that I'd never find it.

I ate strange concoctions and rubbed on even stranger potions. I tried liquid diets like Slimfast and Metrecal. I agreed to be hypnotized. I tried reflexology and even had an acupuncture device stuck in my ear!

Does my story sound a lot like yours? I'm not surprised. No wonder the weight loss business is a billion-dollar industry!

Every new thing I tried seemed to work—at least at first. And losing that first five or ten pounds would get me so excited, I'd believe that this new miracle diet would, finally, get my weight off for keeps.

Inevitably, though, the initial excitement wore off. The diet's routine and boredom set in, and I quit. I shoved the pills to the back of the medicine chest; pushed the cans of powdered shake mix to the rear of the kitchen cabinets; slid all the program materials out of sight under my bed; and once more I felt like a failure.

Like most dieters, I quickly gained back the weight I'd lost each time, along with a few extra "souvenir" pounds that seemed always to settle around my hips. I'd done the diet-lose-weight-gain-it-all-back "yo-yo" on the average of once a year. It's no exaggeration to say that over the years I've lost 1,000 pounds—and gained back 1,150 pounds.

Finally, at the age of forty-six I weighed more than I'd ever imagined possible. I'd stopped believing that any diet could work for me. I drowned my sorrows in sacks of cake donuts, and wondered if I'd live long enough to watch my grandchildren grow up.

Something had to change.

I had to change.

Finally, I did.

I'm just over fifty now—and I'm 130 pounds less than my all-time high of close to 300 pounds. I've kept the weight off for more than six years. I'd like to lose another ten pounds, but I'm not obsessed about it. If it takes me the rest of my life to accomplish it, that's okay.

What I *do* care about is never saying hello again to any of those unwanted pounds I said good-bye to!

How did I jump off the roller coaster I was on? For one thing, I finally stopped looking to food to solve my emotional problems. But what really shook me up—and got me started on the path that changed my life—was Operation Desert Storm in early 1991. I sent three children off to the Persian Gulf War—my son-in-law Matt, a medic in Special Forces; my daughter Becky, a full-time college student and member of a medical unit in the Army Reserve; and my son James, a member of the Inactive Army Reserve reactivated as a chemicals expert.

Somehow, knowing that my children were putting their lives on the line got me thinking about my own mortality—and I knew in my heart the last thing they needed while they were overseas was to get a letter from home saying that their mother was ill because of a food-related problem.

The day I drove the third child to the airport to leave for Saudi Arabia, something happened to me that would change my life for the better—and forever. I stopped praying my constant prayer as a professional dieter, which was simply, "Please, God, let me lose ten pounds by Friday." Instead, I began praying, "God, please help me not be a burden to my kids and my family."

I quit praying for what I wanted, and started praying for what I needed—and in the process my prayers were answered. I couldn't keep the kids safe—that was out of my hands—but I could try to get healthier to better handle the stress of it. It was the least I could do on the homefront.

That quiet prayer was the beginning of the new JoAnna Lund. My initial goal was not to lose weight or create healthy recipes. I only wanted to become healthier for my kids, my husband, and myself.

Each of my children returned safely from the Persian Gulf War. But something didn't come back—the 130 extra pounds I'd been lugging around for far too long. I'd finally accepted the truth after all those agonizing years of suffering through on-again, off-again dieting.

There are no "magic" cures in life.

No "magic" potion, pill, or diet will make unwanted pounds disappear.

I found something better than magic, if you can believe it. When I turned my weight and health dilemma over to God for guidance, a new JoAnna Lund and Healthy Exchanges were born.

I discovered a new way to live my life—and uncovered an unexpected talent for creating easy "common folk" healthy recipes and sharing my commonsense approach to healthy living. I learned that I could motivate others to change their lives and adopt a positive outlook. I began publishing cookbooks and a monthly food newsletter, and speaking to groups all over the country.

I like to say, *"When life handed me a lemon, not only did I make healthy, tasty lemonade, I wrote the recipe down!"*

What I finally found was not a quick fix or a short-term diet, but a great way to live well for a lifetime.

I want to share it with you.

Healthy Exchanges®

Weight Loss

Choices™/Exchanges

If you've ever been on one of the national weight-loss programs like Weight Watchers or Diet Center, you've already been introduced to the concept of measured portions of different food groups that make up your daily food plan. If you are not familiar with such a system of weight-loss choices or exchanges, here's a brief explanation. (If you want or need more detailed information, you can write to the American Dietetic Association or the American Diabetes Association for comprehensive explanations.)

The idea of food exchanges is to divide foods into basic food groups. The foods in each group are measured in servings that have comparable values. These groups include Proteins/Meats, Breads/Starches, Vegetables, Fats, Fruits, Skim Milk, Free Foods, and Optional Calories.

Each choice or exchange included in a particular group has about the same number of calories and a similar carbohydrate, protein, and fat content as the other foods in that group. Because any food on a particular list can be "exchanged" for any other food in that group, it makes sense to call the food groups *exchanges* or *choices*.

I like to think we are also "exchanging" bad habits and food choices for good ones!

By using Weight Loss Choices™ or exchanges you can choose from a variety of foods without having to calculate the nutrient value of each one. This makes it easier to include a wide variety of foods in your daily menus and gives you the opportunity to tailor your choices to your unique appetite.

If you want to lose weight, you should consult your physician or other weight-control expert regarding the number of servings that would be best for you from each food group. Since men generally require more calories than women, and since the requirements for growing children and teenagers differ from those of adults, the right number of exchanges for any one person is a personal decision.

I have included a suggested plan of weight-loss choices in the pages following the exchange lists. It's a program I used to lose 130 pounds, and it's the one I still follow today.

(If you are a diabetic or have been diagnosed with heart problems, it is best to meet with your physician before using this or any other food program or recipe collection.)

Food Group Weight Loss Choices/Exchanges

Not all food group exchanges are alike. The ones that follow are for anyone who's interested in weight loss or maintenance. If you are a diabetic, you should check with your health-care provider or dietitian to get the information you need to help you plan your diet. Diabetic exchanges are calculated by the American Diabetic Association, and information about them is provided in *The Diabetic's Healthy Exchange Cookbook* (Perigee Books).

Every Healthy Exchanges recipe provides calculations in three ways:

- Weight Loss Choices/Exchanges
- Calories, Fat, Protein, Carbohydrates, and Fiber Grams, and Sodium in milligrams
- Diabetic Exchanges calculated for me by a Registered Dietitian

Healthy Exchanges recipes can help you eat well and recover your health, whatever your health concerns may be. Please take a few minutes to review the exchange lists and the suggestions that follow on how to count them. You have lots of great eating in store for you!

Proteins

Meat, poultry, seafood, eggs, cheese, and legumes.

One exchange of Protein is approximately 60 calories. Examples of one Protein choice or exchange:

1 ounce cooked weight of lean meat, poultry, or seafood
2 ounces white fish
1½ ounces 97% fat-free ham
1 egg (limit to no more than 4 per week)
¼ cup egg substitute
3 egg whites
¾ ounce reduced-fat cheese
½ cup fat-free cottage cheese
2 ounces cooked or ¾ ounces uncooked dry beans
1 tablespoon peanut butter (also count 1 fat exchange)

Breads

Breads, crackers, cereals, grains, and starchy vegetables. One exchange of Bread is approximately 80 calories. Examples of one Bread choice/exchange:

1 slice bread or 2 slices reduced-calorie bread (40 calories or less)
1 roll, any type (1 ounce)
½ cup cooked pasta or ¾ ounce uncooked (scant ½ cup)
½ cup cooked rice or 1 ounce uncooked (⅓ cup)
3 tablespoons flour
¾ ounce cold cereal
½ cup cooked hot cereal or ¾ ounce uncooked (2 tablespoons)
½ cup corn (kernels or cream style) or peas
4 ounces white potato, cooked, or 5 ounces uncooked
3 ounces sweet potato, cooked, or 4 ounces uncooked
3 cups air-popped popcorn
7 fat-free crackers (¾ ounce)
3 (2½-inch squares) graham crackers
2 (¾-ounce) rice cakes or 6 mini
1 tortilla, any type (6-inch diameter)

Fruits

All fruits and fruit juices. One exchange of Fruit is approximately 60 calories. Examples of one Fruit choice or exchange:

1 small apple or ½ cup slices
1 small orange
½ medium banana
¾ cup berries (except strawberries and cranberries)
1 cup strawberries or cranberries
½ cup canned fruit, packed in fruit juice or rinsed well
2 tablespoons raisins
1 tablespoon spreadable fruit spread
½ cup apple juice (4 fluid ounces)
½ cup orange juice (4 fluid ounces)
½ cup applesauce

Skim Milk

Milk, buttermilk, and yogurt. One exchange of Skim Milk is approximately 90 calories. Examples of one Skim Milk choice or exchange:

1 cup skim milk
½ cup evaporated skim milk
1 cup low-fat buttermilk
¾ cup plain fat-free yogurt
⅓ cup nonfat dry milk powder

Vegetables

All fresh, canned, or frozen vegetables other than the starchy vegetables. One exchange of Vegetables is approximately 30 calories. Examples of one Vegetable choice or exchange:

½ cup vegetable
¼ cup tomato sauce
1 medium fresh tomato
½ cup vegetable juice

Fats

Margarine, mayonnaise, vegetable oils, salad dressings, olives, and nuts. One exchange of fat is approximately 40 calories. Examples of one Fat choice or exchange:

- 1 teaspoon margarine or 2 teaspoons reduced-calorie margarine
- 1 teaspoon butter
- 1 teaspoon vegetable oil
- 1 teaspoon mayonnaise or 2 teaspoons reduced-calorie mayonnaise
- 1 teaspoon peanut butter
- 1 ounce olives
- ¼ ounce pecans or walnuts

Free Foods

Foods that do not provide nutritional value but are used to enhance the taste of foods are included in the Free Foods group. Examples of these are spices, herbs, extracts, vinegar, lemon juice, mustard, Worcestershire sauce, and soy sauce. Cooking sprays and artificial sweeteners used in moderation are also included in this group. However, you'll see that I include the caloric value of artificial sweeteners in the Optional Calories of the recipes.

You may occasionally see a recipe that lists "free food" as part of the portion. According to the published exchange lists, a free food contains fewer than 20 calories per serving. Two or three servings per day of free foods/drinks are usually allowed in a meal plan.

Optional Calories

Foods that do not fit into any other group but are used in moderation in recipes are included in Optional Calories. Foods that are counted in this way include sugar-free gelatin and puddings, fat-free mayonnaise and dressings, reduced-calorie whipped toppings, reduced-calorie syrups and jams, chocolate chips, coconut, and canned broth.

Sliders™

These are 80 Optional Calorie increments that do not fit into any particular category. You can choose which food groups to *slide* them into. It is wise to limit this selection to approximately three per day to ensure the best possible nutrition for your body while still enjoying an occasional treat.

Sliders may be used in either of the following ways:

1. If you have consumed all your Protein, Bread, Fruit, or Skim Milk Weight Loss Choices for the day, and you want to eat additional foods from those food groups, you simply use a Slider. It's what I call "healthy horse trading." Remember that Sliders may not be traded for choices in the Vegetables or Fats food groups.

2. Sliders may also be deducted from your Optional Calories (OC) for the day or week. ¼ Sl equals 20 OC; ½ Sl equals 40 OC; ¾ Sl equals 60 OC; and 1 Sl equals 80 OC. This way, you can choose the food group to *slide* into.

Healthy Exchanges
Weight Loss Choices

Here's my suggested program of Weight Loss Choices, based on an average daily total of 1,400–1,600 calories per day. *If you require more or fewer calories, please revise this plan to your individual needs.*

Each day, women should plan to eat:

2 Skim Milk servings, 90 calories each
2 Fat servings, 40 calories each
3 Fruit servings, 60 calories each
4 Vegetable servings or more, 30 calories each
5 Protein servings, 60 calories each
5 Bread servings, 80 calories each

Men should add to this basic program: 2 Fat servings (for a total of 4), 1 Protein serving (for a total of 6), and 2 Bread servings (for a total of 7).

Young people should follow the program for Men but add 1 Skim Milk serving for a total of 3 servings.

You may also choose to add up to 100 Optional Calories per day, and up to 28 Sliders per week at 80 calories each. If you choose to include more Sliders in your daily or weekly totals, deduct those 80 calories from your Optional Calorie "bank."

A word about **Sliders**. These are to be counted toward your totals after you have used your allotment of choices of Skim Milk, Protein, Bread, and Fruit for the day. By "sliding" an additional choice into one of these groups, you can meet your individual needs for that day. Sliders are especially helpful when traveling, stressed out, eating out, or for special events. I often use mine so I can enjoy my favorite Healthy Exchanges desserts. Vegetables are not to be counted as Sliders. Enjoy as many Vegetable choices as you need to feel satisfied. Because we want to limit our fat intake to moderate amounts, additional Fat choices should not be counted as Sliders. If you choose to include more fat on an *occasional* basis, count the extra choices as Optional Calories.

Keep a daily food diary of your Weight Loss Choices, checking off what you eat as you go. If, at the end of the day, your required selections are not 100 percent accounted for, but you have done the best you could, go to bed with a clear conscience. There will be days when you have ¼ Fruit or ½ Bread left over. What are you going to do—eat two slices of an orange or half a slice of bread and throw the rest out? I always say that "nothing in life comes out exact." Just do the best you can . . . *the best you can.*

Try to drink at least eight glasses of water a day. Water truly is the "nectar" of good health.

As a little added insurance, I take a multivitamin each day. It's not essential, but if my day's worth of well-planned meals "bites the dust" when unexpected events intrude on my regular routine, my body still gets its vital nutrients.

The calories listed in each group of choices are averages. Some choices within each group may be higher or lower, so it's important to select a variety of different foods instead of eating the same three or four all the time.

Use your Optional Calories! They are what I call "life's little extras." They make all the difference in how you enjoy your food and appreciate the variety available to you. Yes, we can get by without them, but do you really want to? Keep in mind that you should be using all your daily Weight Loss Choices first to ensure you are getting the basics of good nutrition. But I guarantee that Optional Calories will keep you from feeling deprived—and help you reach your weight-loss goals.

Sodium, Fat, Cholesterol, and Processed Foods

A re Healthy Exchanges Ingredients Really Healthy?
When I first created Healthy Exchanges, many people asked about sodium, about whether it was necessary to calculate the percentage of fat, saturated fat, and cholesterol in a healthy diet, and about my use of processed foods in many recipes. I researched these questions as I was developing my program, so you can feel confident about using the recipes and food plan.

Sodium

Most people consume more sodium than their bodies need. The American Heart Association and the American Diabetes Association recommend limiting daily sodium intake to no more than 3,000 mg. per day. If your doctor suggests you limit your sodium even more, then *you really must read labels.*

Sodium is an essential nutrient and should not be completely eliminated. It helps to regulate blood volume and is needed for normal daily muscle and nerve functions. Most of us, however, have no trouble getting "all we need" and then some.

As with everything else, moderation is my approach. I rarely ever have salt in my list as an added ingredient. But if you're especially sodium sensitive, make the right choices for you—and save high-sodium foods such as sauerkraut for an occasional treat.

I use lots of spices to enhance flavors, so you won't notice the absence of salt. In the few cases where it is used, it's vital for the success of the recipe, so please don't omit it.

When I do use an ingredient high in sodium, I try to compensate by using low-sodium products in the remainder of the recipe. Many fat-free products are a little higher in sodium to make up for any flavor that disappeared along with the fat. But when I take advantage of these fat-free, higher-sodium products, I stretch that ingredient within the recipe, lowering the amount of sodium per serving. A good example is my use of fat-free canned soups. While the suggested number of servings per can is two, I make sure my final creation serves at least four and sometimes six. So the soup's sodium has been "watered down" from one-third to one-half of the original amount.

Even if you don't have to watch your sodium intake for medical reasons, using moderation is another "healthy exchange" to make on your own journey to good health.

Fat Percentages

We've been told that 30 percent is the magic number—that we should limit fat intake to 30 percent or less of our total calories. It's good advice, and I try to have a weekly average of 15 to 25 percent myself. I believe any less than 15 percent is really just another restrictive diet that won't last. And more than 25 percent on a regular basis is too much of a good thing.

When I started listing fat grams along with calories in my recipes, I was tempted to include the percentage of calories from fat. After all, in the vast majority of my recipes, that percentage is well below 30 percent. This even includes my pie recipes that allow you a realistic serving instead of many "diet" recipes that tell you a serving is $1/12$ of a pie.

Figuring fat grams is easy enough. Each gram of fat equals nine calories. Multiply fat grams by 9 then divide that number by the total calories to get the percentage of calories from fat.

So why don't I do it? After consulting four registered dietitians for advice, I decided to omit this information. They felt that it's too easy for people to become obsessed by that 30 percent figure, which is after all supposed to be a percentage of total calories over the course of a day or a week. We mustn't feel we can't include a healthy ingredient such as pecans or olives in one recipe just because, on its own, it has more than 30 percent of its calories from fat.

An example of this would be a casserole made with 90 percent lean red meat. Most of us benefit from eating red meat in moderation, as it provides iron and niacin in our diets, and it also makes life more enjoyable for us and those who eat with us. If we *only* look at the percentage of calories from fat in a serving of this one dish, which might be as high as 40 to 45 percent, we might choose not to include this recipe in our weekly food plan.

The dietitians suggested that it's important to consider the total picture when making such decisions. As long as your overall food plan keeps fat calories to 30 percent, it's all right to enjoy an occasional dish that is somewhat higher in fat content. Healthy foods I include in **MODERATION** include 90 percent lean red meat, olives, and nuts. I don't eat these foods every day, and you may not either. But occasionally, in a good recipe, they make all the difference in the world between just getting by (deprivation) and truly enjoying your food.

Remember, the goal is eating in a healthy way so you can enjoy and live well the rest of your life.

Saturated Fats and Cholesterol

You'll see that I don't provide calculations for saturated fats or cholesterol amounts in my recipes. It's for the simple and yet not so simple reason that accurate, up-to-date, brand-specific information can be difficult to obtain from food manufacturers, especially since the way in which they produce food keeps changing rapidly. But once more I've consulted with registered dietitians and other professionals and found that because I use only a few products that are high in saturated fat, and use them in such limited quantities, my recipes are suitable for patients concerned about controlling or lowering cholesterol. You'll also find that whenever I do use one of these ingredients *in moderation*, everything else in the recipe, and in the meals my family and I enjoy, is low in fat.

Processed Foods

Some people have asked how "healthy" recipes can so often use "processed foods"—ready-made products like canned soups, prepared piecrusts, frozen potatoes, and frozen whipped topping? Well, I believe that such foods, used properly (that word **moderation** again) as part of a healthy lifestyle, have a place as ingredients in healthy recipes.

I'm not in favor of spraying everything we eat with chemicals, and I don't mean that all our foods should come out of packages. But I do think we should use the best available products to make cooking easier and foods taste better. I take advantage of good low-fat and low-sugar products, and my recipes are created for busy people like me who want to eat well and eat healthy. I don't expect people to visit out-of-the-way health food stores or find time to cook beans from scratch—*because I don't*. There are lots of very good processed foods available in your local grocery store, and they can make it so much easier to enjoy the benefits of healthy eating.

I certainly don't recommend that everything you eat come from a can, box, or jar. In the best of all possible worlds I would start with the basics: rice, poultry, fish, or beef, and raw vegetables—then throw in a can of reduced-sodium/97 percent fat-free soup (a processed food), and end up with an appetizing, easy-to-prepare, healthy meal.

Most of us can't grow fresh food in the backyard, and many people don't even have a nearby farmer's market. But instead of saying, "Well, I can't get to the health food store so why not eat that hot fudge sundae?" you gotta play ball in your private ball field, not in someone else's. I want to help you figure out ways to make living healthy **doable** and **livable** *wherever you live*, or you're not going to stick with it.

I've checked with the American Dietetic Association, the American Diabetes Association, and with many registered dietitians, and

I've been assured that sugar-free and fat-free processed products that use substitutes for sugar and fat are safe when used in the intended way. This means a realistic serving, not one hundred cans of diet soda every day of the year! Even carrots can turn your skin orange if you eat far too many, but does anyone suggest we avoid eating carrots?

Of course, it is your privilege to disagree with me and to use whatever you choose when you prepare your food. I never want to be one of those "opinionated" people who think it's their God-given right to make personal decisions for others and insist that their way is the *only* way.

Besides, new research comes out every day that declares one food bad and another food good. Then a few days later, some new information emerges, saying that the opposite is true. When the facts are sifted from the fiction, the truth is probably somewhere in between. I know I feel confused when what was bad for you last year is good for you now, and vice versa.

Instead of listening to unreasonable sermons by naysayers who are nowhere around when it comes time to make a quick and healthy meal for your family, I've tried to incorporate the best processed foods I can find into my Healthy Exchanges recipes. I get stacks of mail from people who are thrilled to discover they can eat good-tasting food and who proudly use processed foods in the intended way. I think you will agree that my commonsense approach to healthy cooking is the right choice for many. Because these foods are convenient, tasty, and good substitutes for less healthy products, people are willing to use them long-term.

So don't let anyone make you feel ashamed for including these products in your healthy lifestyle. Only you can decide what's best for you and your family's needs. Part of living a healthy lifestyle is making those decisions and *getting on with life*.

JoAnna's Ten Commandments of Successful Cooking

A few minutes spent before you start cooking will save you hours in the kitchen. The best use of your time, energy, and money is not only reading these suggestions for conquering the kitchen but also applying them to your daily cooking.

1. **Read the entire recipe from start to finish** and be sure you understand the process involved. Check that you have all the equipment you will need *before* you begin.

2. **Check the ingredient list** and be sure you have *everything* and in the amounts required. Keep cooking sprays handy—while they're not listed as ingredients, I use them all the time (just a quick squirt!).

3. **Set out *all* the ingredients and equipment needed** to prepare the recipe on the counter near you *before* you start. Remember that old saying, *A stitch in time saves nine.* It applies in the kitchen, too.

4. **Do as much advance preparation as possible** before actually cooking. Chop, cut, grate, or do whatever is needed to prepare the ingredients and have them ready before you start to mix. Turn the oven on at least ten minutes before putting food in to bake, to allow the oven to preheat to the proper temperature.

5. **Use a kitchen timer** to tell you when the cooking or baking time is up. Because stove temperatures vary slightly by manufacturer, you may want to set your timer for five minutes less than the suggested time just to prevent overcooking. Check the progress of your dish at that time, then decide if you need the additional minutes or not.

6. **Measure carefully.** Use glass measures for liquids and metal or plastic cups for dry ingredients. My recipes are based on standard measurements. Unless I tell you it's a scant or full cup, measure the cup level.

7. **For best results, follow the recipe instructions exactly.** Feel free to substitute ingredients that *don't tamper* with the basic chemistry of the recipe, but be sure to leave key ingredients alone. For example, you could substitute sugar-free instant chocolate pudding for sugar-free instant butterscotch pudding, but if you used a six-serving package when a four-serving package was listed in the ingredients, or you used instant when cook-and-serve is required, you won't get the right result.

8. **Clean up as you go.** It is much easier to wash a few items at a time than to face a whole counter of dirty dishes later. The same is true for spills on the counter or floor.

9. **Be careful about doubling or halving a recipe.** Though many recipes can be altered successfully to serve more or fewer people, *many cannot.* This is especially true when it comes to spices and liquids. If you try to double a recipe that calls for one teaspoon of pumpkin-pie spice, for example, and you double the spice, you may end up with a too-spicy taste. I usually suggest increasing spices or liquid by 1½ times when doubling a recipe. If it tastes a little bland to you, you can increase the spice to 1¾ times the original amount the next time you prepare the dish. Remember you can always add more, but you can't take it out after it's been stirred in.

The same is true with liquid ingredients. If you wanted to triple a recipe like my Macho Burritos because you were planning to serve a crowd, you might think you should use three times as much of every ingredient. Don't, or you could end up with Burrito Soup! The original recipe calls for 1¾ cups of chunky tomato sauce, so I'd suggest using 3½ cups of sauce when you triple the recipe (or 2¾ cups if you double it). You'll still have a good-tasting dish that won't run all over the plate.

10. **Write your reactions next to each recipe once you've served it.** Yes, that's right, I'm giving you permission to write in this book. It's yours, after all. Ask yourself: Did everyone like it? Did I have to add another half teaspoon of chili seasoning to please my family, who like to live on the spicier side of the street? You may even want to rate the recipe on a scale of 1★ to 4★, depending on what you thought of it. (Four stars would be the top rating—and I hope you'll feel that way about many of my recipes.) Jotting down your comments while they are fresh in your mind will help you personalize the recipe to your own taste the next time you prepare it.

My Best Healthy Exchanges Tips and Tidbits

Measurements, General Cooking Tips, and Basic Ingredients

The word **moderation** best describes **my use of fats, sugar substitutes**, and **sodium** in these recipes. Wherever possible, I've used cooking spray for sautéing and for browning meats and vegetables. I also use reduced-calorie margarine and no-fat mayonnaise and salad dressings. Lean ground turkey *or* ground beef can be used in the recipes. Just be sure whatever you choose is at least *90 percent lean.*

I've also included **small amounts of sugar and brown sugar substitutes as the sweetening agent** in many of the recipes. I don't drink a hundred cans of soda a day or eat enough artificially sweetened foods in a twenty-four-hour time period to be troubled by sugar substitutes. But if this is a concern of yours and you *do not* need to watch your sugar intake, you can always replace the sugar substitutes with processed sugar and the sugar-free products with regular ones.

I created my recipes knowing they would also be used by hypoglycemics, diabetics, and those concerned about triglycerides. If you choose to use sugar instead, be sure to count the additional calories.

A word of caution when cooking with *sugar substitutes*: Use *saccharin*-based sweeteners when *heating or baking*. In recipes that **don't require heat, Aspartame** (known as NutraSweet) works well in uncooked dishes but leaves an aftertaste in baked products.

I'm often asked why I use an **8-by-8-inch baking dish** in my recipes. It's for portion control. If the recipe says it serves four, just cut down the center, turn the dish, and cut again. Like magic, there's your serving. Also, if this is the only recipe you are preparing requiring an oven, the square dish fits into a tabletop toaster oven easily and energy can be conserved.

To make life even easier, **whenever a recipe calls for ounce measurements** (other than raw meats) I've included the closest cup equivalent. I need to use my scale daily when creating recipes, so I've measured for you at the same time.

Most of the recipes are for **4 to 6 servings**. If you don't have that many to feed, do what I do: freeze individual portions. Then all you have to do is choose something from the freezer and take it to work for lunch or have your evening meals prepared in advance for the week. In this way, I always have something on hand that is both good to eat and good for me.

Unless a recipe includes hard-boiled eggs, cream cheese, mayonnaise, or a raw vegetable or fruit, **the leftovers should freeze well**. (I've marked recipes that freeze well with the symbol of a **snowflake ❅**.) This includes most of the cream pies. Divide any recipe up into individual servings and freeze for your own "TV" dinners.

Another good idea is **cutting leftover pie into individual pieces and freezing each one separately** in a small Ziploc freezer bag. Then the next time you want to thaw a piece of pie for yourself, you don't have to thaw the whole pie. It's great this way for brown-bag lunches, too. Just pull a piece out of the freezer on your way to work and by lunchtime you will have a wonderful dessert waiting for you.

Unless I specify **"covered" for simmering or baking**, prepare my recipes **uncovered**. Occasionally you will read a recipe that asks you to cover a dish for a time, then to uncover, so read the directions carefully to avoid confusion—and to get the best results.

Low-fat cooking spray is another blessing in a Healthy Exchanges kitchen. It's currently available in three flavors . . .

* OLIVE OIL–FLAVORED when cooking Mexican, Italian, or Greek dishes
* BUTTER FLAVORED when the hint of butter is desired
* REGULAR for everything else

A quick spray of the butter-flavored kind makes air-popped popcorn a low-fat taste treat, or try it as a butter substitute on steaming hot corn on the cob. One light spray of the skillet when browning meat will convince you that you're using "old fashioned fat," and a quick coating of the casserole dish before you add the ingredients will make serving easier and cleanup quicker.

I use reduced-sodium **canned chicken broth** in place of dry bouillon to lower the sodium content. The intended flavor is still present in the prepared dish. As a reduced-sodium beef broth is not currently available (at least not in DeWitt, Iowa), I use the canned regular beef broth. The sodium content is still lower than regular dry bouillon.

Whenever **cooked rice or pasta** is an ingredient, follow the package directions, but eliminate the salt and/or margarine called for. This helps lower the sodium and fat content. It tastes just fine; trust me on this.

Here's another tip: When **cooking rice or noodles**, why not cook extra "for the pot"? After you use what you need, store leftover rice in a covered container (where it will keep for a couple of days). With noodles like spaghetti or macaroni, first rinse and drain as usual, then measure out what you need. Put the leftovers, covered with water, in a bowl, then store in the refrigerator, covered, until they're needed. Then, measure out what you need, rinse and drain them, and they're ready to go.

Does your **pita bread** often tear before you can make a sandwich? Here's my tip to make it open easily: cut the bread in half, put the halves in the microwave for about 15 seconds, and they will open up by themselves. Voilà!

When **chunky salsa** is listed as an ingredient, I leave the degree of "heat" up to your personal taste. In our house, I'm considered a wimp. I go for the "mild" while Cliff prefers "extra-hot." How do we compromise? I prepare the recipe with mild salsa because he can always add a spoonful or two of the hotter version to his serving, but I can't enjoy the dish if it's too spicy for me.

Proteins

I use eggs in moderation. I enjoy the real thing on an average of three to four times a week. So, my recipes are calculated on using whole eggs. However, if you choose to use egg substitutes in place of the egg, the finished product will turn out just fine and the fat grams per serving will be even lower than those listed.

If you like the look, taste, and feel of **hard-boiled eggs** in salads but haven't been using them because of the cholesterol in the yolk, I have a couple of alternatives for you. (1) Pour an 8-ounce carton of egg substitute into a medium skillet sprayed with cooking spray. Cover skillet tightly and cook over low heat until substitute is just set, about 10 minutes. Remove from heat and let set, still covered, for 10 minutes more. Uncover and cool completely. Chop set mixture. This will make about 1 cup of chopped egg. (2) Even easier is to hard-boil "real eggs," toss the yolk away, and chop the white. Either way, you don't deprive yourself of the pleasure of egg in your salad.

In most recipes calling for **egg substitutes**, you can use 2 egg whites in place of the equivalent of 1 egg substitute. Just break the eggs open and toss the yolks away. I can hear some of you already saying, "But that's wasteful!" Well, take a look at the price on the egg substitute package (which usually has the equivalent of 4 eggs in it), then look at the price of a dozen eggs, from which you'd get the equivalent of 6 egg substitutes. Now, what's wasteful about that?

Whenever I include **cooked chicken** in a recipe, I use roasted white meat without skin. Whenever I include **roast beef or pork** in a recipe, I use the loin cuts because they are much leaner. However, most of the time, I do my roasting of all these meats at the local deli. I just ask for a chunk of their lean roasted meat, 6 or 8 ounces, and ask them to slice it. When I get home, I cube or dice the meat and am ready to use it in my recipe. The reason I do this is threefold. (1) I'm getting just the amount I need without leftovers. (2) I don't have the expense of heating the oven. (3) I'm not throwing away the bone, gristle, and fat I'd be cutting away from the meat. Overall, it is probably cheaper to "roast" it the way I do.

Did you know that you can make an acceptable meat loaf without using egg for the binding? Just replace every egg with ¼ cup of liquid. You could use beef broth, tomato sauce, even applesauce, to name just a few alternatives. For a meat loaf to serve six, I always use one pound of extra-lean ground beef or turkey, six tablespoons of dried fine bread crumbs, and ¼ cup of the liquid, plus anything else healthy that strikes my fancy at the time. I mix well and place the mixture in an 8-by-8-inch baking dish or 9-by-5-inch loaf pan sprayed with cooking spray. Bake uncovered at 350 degrees for 35 to 50 minutes (depending on the added ingredients). You will never miss the egg.

Anytime you are **browning ground meat** for a casserole and want to get rid of almost all of the excess fat, just place the uncooked meat loosely in a plastic colander. Set the colander in a glass pie plate. Place in a microwave and cook on High for three to six minutes (depending on the amount being browned), stirring often. Use as you would for any casserole. You can also chop up onions and brown them with the meat if you want to.

Milk and Yogurt

Take it from me—nonfat dry milk powder is great! I *do not* use it for drinking, but I *do* use it for cooking. Three good reasons why:

1. It is very **inexpensive**.

2. It does not sour because you use it only as needed. Store the box in your refrigerator or freezer and it will keep almost forever.

3. You can easily **add extra calcium** to just about any recipe without added liquid.

I consider nonfat dry milk powder one of Mother Nature's modern-day miracles of convenience. But do purchase a good national name brand (I like Carnation), and keep it fresh by proper storage.

In many of my pies and puddings, I use nonfat dry milk powder and water instead of skim milk. Usually I call for ²/₃ cup nonfat dry milk powder and 1¼ to 1½ cups water or liquid. This way I can get the nutrients of two cups of milk, but much less liquid, and the end result is much creamier. Also, the recipe sets up more quickly, usually in 5 minutes or less. So if someone knocks at your door unexpectedly at mealtime, you can quickly throw a pie together and enjoy it minutes later.

You can make your own "**sour cream**" by combining ¾ cup plain fat-free yogurt with ⅓ cup nonfat dry milk powder. What you did by doing this is fourfold: (1) The dry milk stabilizes the yogurt and keeps the whey from separating. (2) The dry milk slightly helps to cut the tartness of the yogurt. (3) It's still virtually fat-free. (4) The calcium has been increased by 100 percent. Isn't it great how we can make that distant relative of sour cream a first kissin' cousin by adding the nonfat dry milk powder? Or, if you place 1 cup of plain fat-free yogurt in a sieve lined with a coffee filter, and place the sieve over a small bowl and refrigerate for about 6 hours, you will end up with a very good alternative for sour cream. To **stabilize yogurt** when cooking or baking with it, just add 1 teaspoon cornstarch to every ¾ cup yogurt.

If a recipe calls for **evaporated skim milk** and you don't have any in the cupboard, make your own. For every ½ cup evaporated skim milk needed, combine ⅓ cup nonfat dry milk powder and ½ cup water. Use as you would evaporated skim milk.

You can also make your own **sugar-free and fat-free sweetened condensed milk** at home. Combine 1⅓ cups nonfat dry milk powder and ½ cup cold water in a 2-cup glass measure. Cover and microwave on High until mixture is hot but *not* boiling. Stir in ½ cup Sprinkle Sweet or Sugar Twin. Cover and refrigerate at least 4 hours. This mixture will keep for up to two weeks in the refrigerator. Use in just about any recipe that calls for sweetened condensed milk.

For any recipe that calls for **buttermilk**, you might want to try Jo's Buttermilk: Blend one cup of water and ²/₃ cup dry milk powder (the nutrients of two cups of skim milk). It'll be thicker than this mixed-up milk usually is, because it's doubled. Add 1 teaspoon white vinegar and stir, then let it sit for at least ten minutes.

One of my subscribers was looking for a way to further restrict salt intake and needed a substitute for **cream of mushroom soup**. For many of my recipes, I use Healthy Request Cream of Mushroom soup, as it is a reduced-sodium product. The label suggests two servings per can, but I usually incorporate the soup into a recipe serving at least four. By doing this, I've reduced the sodium in the soup by half again.

But if you must restrict your sodium even more, try making my Healthy Exchanges **Creamy Mushroom Sauce**. Place 1½ cups evaporated skim milk and 3 tablespoons flour in a covered jar. Shake well and pour mixture into a medium saucepan sprayed with butter-flavored cooking spray. Add ½ cup canned sliced mushrooms, rinsed and drained. Cook over medium heat, stirring often, until mixture thickens. Add any seasonings of your choice. You can use this sauce in any recipe that calls for one 10¾-ounce can of cream of mushroom soup.

Why did I choose these proportions and ingredients?

- 1½ cups of evaporated skim milk is the amount in one can.
- It's equal to three milk choices or exchanges.
- It's the perfect amount of liquid and flour for a medium cream sauce.
- Three tablespoons of flour are equal to one Bread/Starch choice or exchange.
- Any leftovers will reheat beautifully with a flour-based sauce, but not with a cornstarch base.
- The mushrooms are one vegetable choice or exchange.
- This sauce is virtually fat free, sugar free, and sodium free.

Fruits and Vegetables

If you want to enjoy a "**fruit shake**" with some pizazz, just combine soda water and unsweetened fruit juice in a blender. Add crushed ice. Blend on High until thick. Refreshment without guilt.

You'll see that many recipes use ordinary **canned vegetables**. They're much cheaper than reduced-sodium versions, and once you rinse and drain them, the sodium is reduced anyway. I believe in saving money wherever possible so we can afford the best in fat-free and sugar-free products as they come onto the market.

All three kinds of **vegetables—fresh, frozen, and canned—** have their place in a healthy diet. My husband, Cliff, hates the taste of frozen or fresh green beans, thinks the texture is all wrong, so I use canned green beans instead. In this case, canned vegetables have their proper place when I'm feeding my husband. If someone in your family has a similar concern, it's important to respond to it so everyone can be happy and enjoy the meal.

When I use **fruits or vegetables** like apples, cucumbers, and zucchini, I wash them really well and **leave their skin on**. It provides added color, fiber, and attractiveness to any dish. And, because I use processed flour in my cooking, I like to increase the fiber in my diet by eating my fruits and vegetables in their closest-to-natural state.

To help keep **fresh fruits and veggies fresh**, just give them a quick "shower" with lemon juice. The easiest way to do this is to pour purchased lemon juice into a kitchen spray bottle and store in the refrigerator. Then, every time you use fresh fruits or vegetables in a salad or dessert, simply give them a quick spray with your "lemon spritzer." You just might be amazed by how well this little trick keeps your produce from turning brown so fast.

The next time you warm canned vegetables such as carrots or green beans, drain and heat the vegetables in ¼ cup beef or chicken broth. It gives a nice variation to an old standby. Here's how a simple **white sauce** for vegetables and casseroles can be made without using added fat by spraying a medium saucepan with butter-flavored cooking spray: Place 1½ cups evaporated skim milk and 3 tablespoons flour in a covered jar. Shake well. Pour into sprayed saucepan and cook over medium heat until thick, stirring constantly. Add salt and pepper to taste. You can also add ½ cup canned drained mushrooms and/or 3 ounces (¾ cup) shredded reduced-fat cheese. Continue cooking until cheese melts.

Zip up canned or frozen green beans with **chunky salsa**: ½ cup to 2 cups beans. Heat thoroughly. Chunky salsa also makes a wonderful dressing on lettuce salads. It only counts as a vegetable, so enjoy.

Another wonderful **South of the Border** dressing can be stirred up by using ½ cup of chunky salsa and ¼ cup of fat-free Ranch dressing. Cover and store in your refrigerator. Use as a dressing for salads or as a topping for baked potatoes.

For **gravy** with all the "old time" flavor but without the extra fat, try this almost effortless way to prepare it. (It's almost as easy as opening up a store-bought jar.) Pour the juice off your roasted meat, then set the roast aside to "rest" for about 20 minutes. Place the juice in an uncovered cake pan or other large flat pan (we want the large air surface to speed up the cooling process) and put it in the freezer until the fat congeals on top and you can skim it off. Or, if you prefer, use a skimming pitcher purchased at your kitchen gadget store. Either way, measure about 1½ cups skimmed broth and pour into a medium saucepan. Cook over medium heat until heated through, about five minutes. In a covered jar, combine ½ cup water or cooled potato broth with 3 tablespoons flour. Shake well. Pour flour mixture into warmed juice. Combine well using a wire whisk. Continue cooking until gravy thickens, about 5 minutes. Season with salt and pepper to taste.

Why did I use flour instead of cornstarch? Because any leftovers will reheat nicely with the flour base and would not with a cornstarch base. Also, 3 tablespoons of flour works out to 1 Bread/Starch exchange. This virtually fat-free gravy makes about 2 cups, so you could spoon about ½ cup gravy on your low-fat mashed potatoes and only have to count your gravy as ¼ Bread/Starch exchange.

Desserts

Thaw **lite whipped topping** in the refrigerator overnight. Never try to force the thawing by stirring or using a microwave to soften. Stirring it will remove the air from the topping that gives it the lightness and texture we want, and there's not enough fat in it to survive being heated.

How can I **frost an entire pie with just ½ cup of whipped topping?** First, don't use an inexpensive brand. I use Cool Whip Lite or La Creme lite. Make sure the topping is fully thawed. Always spread from the center to the sides using a rubber spatula. This way, ½ cup topping will literally cover an entire pie. Remember, the operative word is **frost**, not pile the entire container on top of the pie!

Here's a way to **extend the flavor (and oils) of purchased whipped topping:** Blend together ¾ cup plain nonfat yogurt and ⅓ cup nonfat dry milk powder. Add sugar substitute to equal 2 tablespoons sugar, 1 cup Cool Whip Lite and 1 teaspoon of the flavoring of your choice (vanilla, coconut, or almond are all good choices). Gently mix and use as you would whipped topping. The texture is almost a cross between marshmallow cream and whipped cream. This is enough to mound high on a pie.

For a different taste when preparing sugar-free instant pudding mixes, use ¾ cup plain fat-free yogurt for one of the required cups of milk. Blend as usual. It will be *thicker and creamier*. And, no it doesn't taste like yogurt. Another variation for the sugar-free instant vanilla pudding is to use 1 cup skim milk and 1 cup crushed pineapple juice. Mix as usual.

For a special treat that tastes anything but "diet," try placing **spreadable fruit** in a container and microwave for about 15 seconds. Then pour the melted fruit spread over a serving of nonfat ice cream or frozen yogurt. One tablespoon of spreadable fruit is equal to 1 fruit serving. Some combinations to get you started are apricot over chocolate ice cream, strawberry over strawberry ice cream, or any flavor over vanilla. Another way I use spreadable fruit is to make a delicious **topping for a cheesecake or angel food cake.** I take ½ cup of fruit and ½ cup Cool Whip Lite and blend the two together with a teaspoon of coconut extract.

Here's a really **good topping** for the fall of the year. Place 1½ cups of unsweetened applesauce in a medium saucepan or 4-cup glass measure. Stir in two tablespoons of raisins, 1 teaspoon of apple-pie spice, and two tablespoons of Cary's sugar-free maple syrup. Cook over medium heat on the stove or process on High in the microwave until warm. Then spoon about ½ cup of the warm mixture over pancakes, French toast, or fat-free and sugar-free vanilla ice cream. It's as close as you will get to guilt-free apple pie!

A quick yet tasty way to prepare **strawberries for shortcake** is to place about ¾ cup of sliced strawberries, 2 tablespoons of Diet Mountain Dew, and sugar substitute to equal ¼ cup sugar in a blender container. Process on Blend until the mixture is smooth. Pour the mixture into a bowl. Add 1¼ cups of sliced strawberries and mix well. Cover and refrigerate until ready to serve with shortcakes.

The next time you are making treats for the family, try using **unsweetened applesauce** for some or all of the required oil in the recipe. For instance, if the recipe calls for ½ cup of cooking oil, use up to the ½ cup in applesauce. It works and most people will not even notice the difference. It's great in purchased cake mixes, but so far I haven't been able to figure out a way to deep-fat fry with it!

Another trick I often use is to include tiny amounts of "real people" food, such as coconut, but extend the flavor by using extracts. Try it—you will be surprised by how little of the real thing you can use and still feel you are not being deprived.

If you are preparing a pie filling that has ample moisture, just line **graham crackers** in the bottom of a 9-by-9-inch cake pan. Pour the filling over the top of the crackers. Cover and refrigerate until the moisture has had enough time to soften the crackers. Overnight is best. This eliminates the added **fats and sugars of a piecrust**.

When **stirring fat-free cream cheese to soften it**, use only a sturdy spoon, never an electric mixer. The speed of a mixer can cause the cream cheese to lose its texture and become watery.

Did you know you can make your own **fruit-flavored yogurt?** Mix 1 tablespoon of any flavor of spreadable fruit spread with ¾ cup of plain yogurt. It's every bit as tasty and much cheaper. You can also make your own **lemon yogurt** by combining 3 cups of plain fat-free yogurt with 1 tub of Crystal Light lemonade powder. Mix well, cover, and store in the refrigerator. I think you will be pleasantly surprised by the ease, cost, and flavor of this "made from scratch" calcium-rich treat. P.S.: You can make any flavor you like by using any of the Crystal Light mixes—Cranberry? Iced tea? You decide.

Sugar-free puddings and gelatins are important to many of my recipes, but if you prefer to avoid sugar substitutes, you could still prepare the recipes with regular puddings or gelatins. The calories would be higher, but you would still be cooking low-fat.

When a recipe calls for **chopped nuts** (and you only have whole ones), who wants to dirty the food processor just for a couple of tablespoons? You could try to chop them using your cutting board, but be prepared for bits and pieces to fly all over the kitchen. I use "Grandma's food processor." I take the biggest nuts I can find, put them in a small glass bowl, and chop them into chunks just the right size using a metal biscuit cutter.

If you have a **leftover muffin** and are looking for something a little different for breakfast, you can make a **"breakfast sundae."** Crumble the muffin into a cereal bowl. Sprinkle a serving of fresh fruit over it and top with a couple of tablespoons of nonfat plain yogurt sweetened with sugar substitute and your choice of extract. The thought of it just might make you jump out of bed with a smile on your face. (Speaking of muffins, did you know that if you fill the unused muffin wells with water when baking muffins, you help ensure more even baking and protect the muffin pan at the same time?) Another muffin hint: lightly spray the inside of paper baking cups with butter-flavored cooking spray before spooning the muffin batter into them. Then you won't end up with paper clinging to your fresh-baked muffins.

The secret of making **good meringues** without sugar is to use 1 tablespoon of Sprinkle Sweet or Sugar Twin for every egg white, and a small amount of extract. Use ½ to 1 teaspoon for the batch. Almond, vanilla, and coconut are all good choices. Use the same amount of cream of tartar you usually do. Bake the meringue in the same old way. Don't think you can't have meringue pies because you can't eat sugar. You can, if you do it my way. (Remember that egg whites whip up best at room temperature.)

Homemade or Store-Bought?

I've been asked which is better for you, homemade from scratch or purchased foods. My answer is *both*! They each have a place in a healthy lifestyle, and what that place is has everything to do with you.

Take **piecrusts**, for instance. If you love spending your spare time in the kitchen preparing foods, and you're using low-fat, low-sugar, and reasonably low-sodium ingredients, go for it! But if, like so many people, your time is limited and you've learned to read labels, you could be better off using purchased foods.

I know that when I prepare a pie (and I experiment with a couple of pies each week, because this is Cliff's favorite dessert), I use a purchased crust. Why? Mainly because I can't make a good-tasting piecrust that is lower in fat than the brands I use. Also, purchased piecrusts fit my rule of "If it takes longer to cook it than eat it, forget it!"

I've checked the nutrient information for the purchased piecrust against recipes for traditional and "diet" piecrusts, using my computer software program. The purchased crust calculated lower in both fat and calories! I have tried some low-fat and low-sugar recipes, but they just don't spark my taste buds, or were so complicated you needed an engineering degree just to get the crust in the pie plate.

I'm very happy with the purchased piecrusts in my recipes, because the finished product rarely, if ever, has more than 30 percent of total calories coming from fat. I also believe that we have to prepare foods our families and friends will eat with us on a regular basis and not feel deprived, or we've wasted our time, energy, and money.

I could use a purchased "lite" **pie filling**, but instead I make my own. Here I can save both fat and sugar, and still make the filling almost as fast as opening a can. The bottom line: know what you have to spend when it comes to both time and fat/sugar calories, then make the best decision you can for you and your family. And don't go without an occasional piece of pie because you think it isn't *necessary*. A delicious pie prepared in a healthy way is one of the simple pleasures of life. It's a little thing, but it can make all the difference between just getting by with the bare minimum and living a full and healthy lifestyle.

Many people have experimented with my tip about **substituting applesauce and artificial sweetener for butter and sugar**, but what if you aren't satisfied with the result? One woman wrote to me about a recipe for her grandmother's cookies that called for 1 cup of butter and 1½ cups of sugar. Well, any recipe that depends on as much butter and sugar as this one does is generally not a good candidate for "healthy exchanges." The original recipe needed a large quantity of fat to produce the crisp cookies just like the ones Grandma made.

Unsweetened applesauce can be used to substitute for vegetable oil with various degrees of success, but not to replace butter, lard, or margarine. If your recipe calls for ½ cup oil or less, and it's a quick bread, muffin, or bar cookie, replacing the oil with applesauce should work. If the recipe calls for more than ½ cup oil, then experiment with half oil, half applesauce. You've still made the recipe healthier, even if you haven't removed all the oil from it.

Another rule for healthy substitution: up to ½ cup of sugar or less can be replaced by *an artificial sweetener* (like Sugar Twin or Sprinkle Sweet) *that can withstand the heat of baking.* If it requires more than ½ cup sugar, cut the amount needed by 75 percent and use ½ cup sugar substitute and sugar for the rest. Other options: reduce the butter and sugar by 25 percent and see if the finished product still satisfies you in taste and appearance. Or, make the cookies just the way Grandma did, realizing they are part of your family's holiday tradition. Enjoy a moderate serving of a couple of cookies once or twice during the season, and just forget about them the rest of the year.

I'm sure you'll add to this list of cooking tips as you begin preparing Healthy Exchanges recipes and discover how easy it can be to adapt your own favorite recipes using these ideas and your own common sense.

A Peek Into My Pantry and My Favorite Brands

Everyone asks me what foods I keep on hand and what brands I use. There are lots of good products on the grocery shelves today—many more than we dreamed about even a year or two ago. And I can't wait to see what's out there twelve months from now. The following are my staples and, where appropriate, my favorites *at this time*. I feel these products are healthier, tastier, easy to get—and deliver the most flavor for the least amount of fat, sugar, or calories. If you find others you like as well *or better*, please use them. This is only a guide to make your grocery shopping and cooking easier.

Fat-free plain yogurt (*Yoplait*)
Nonfat dry skim milk powder (*Carnation*)
Evaporated skim milk (*Carnation*)
Skim milk
Fat-free cottage cheese
Fat-free cream cheese (*Philadelphia*)
Fat-free mayonnaise (*Kraft*)
Fat-free salad dressings (*Kraft*)
Fat-free sour cream (*Land O Lakes*)
Reduced-calorie margarine (*Weight Watchers, Promise, or Smart Beat*)
Cooking spray:
    Olive oil–flavored and regular (*Pam*)

Butter flavored for sautéing (*Weight Watchers*)

Butter flavored for spritzing *after* cooking (*I Can't Believe It's Not Butter!*)

Vegetable oil (*Puritan Canola Oil*)

Reduced-calorie whipped topping (*Cool Whip Lite*)

Sugar Substitute:

If no heating is involved (*Equal*)

If heating is required:

white (*Sugar Twin or Sprinkle Sweet*)

brown (*Brown Sugar Twin*)

Sugar-free gelatin and pudding mixes (*JELL-O*)

Baking mix (*Bisquick Reduced-Fat*)

Pancake mix (*Aunt Jemima Reduced Calorie*)

Reduced-calorie pancake syrup (*Cary's Sugar Free*)

Parmesan cheese (*Kraft Fat Free or Weight Watchers Fat Free*)

Reduced-fat cheese (*Kraft ⅓ Less Fat and Weight Watchers*)

Shredded frozen potatoes (*Mr. Dell's*)

Spreadable fruit spread (*Smucker's, Welch's or Sorrell Ridge*)

Peanut butter (*Peter Pan Reduced Fat, Jif Reduced Fat, or Skippy Reduced Fat*)

Chicken broth (*Healthy Request*)

Beef broth (*Swanson*)

Tomato sauce (*Hunts—Chunky and Regular*)

Canned soups (*Healthy Request*)

Tomato juice (*Campbell's Reduced Sodium*)

Ketchup (*Heinz Lite Harvest or Healthy Choice*)

Purchased piecrust:

unbaked (*Pillsbury—from dairy case*)

graham cracker, butter flavored, or chocolate flavored (*Keebler*)

Pastrami and corned beef (*Carl Buddig Lean*)

Luncheon meats (*Healthy Choice or Oscar Mayer*)

Ham (*Dubuque 97% fat free and reduced sodium or Healthy Choice*)

Frankfurters and Kielbasa sausage (*Healthy Choice*)

Canned white chicken, packed in water (*Swanson*)

Canned tuna, packed in water (*Starkist*)

90-percent-lean ground turkey and beef

Soda crackers (*Nabisco Fat Free*)

Reduced-calorie bread—40 calories per slice or less
Hamburger buns—80 calories each (*Colonial Old Fashion or Less*)
Rice—instant, regular, brown, and wild
Instant potato flakes (*Betty Crocker Potato Buds*)
Noodles, spaghetti, and macaroni
Salsa (*Chi-Chi's Mild*)
Pickle relish—dill, sweet, and hot dog
Mustard—Dijon, prepared, and spicy
Unsweetened apple juice
Unsweetened applesauce
Fruit—fresh, frozen (no sugar added), or canned in juice
Vegetables—fresh, frozen, or canned
Spices—JO's Spices
Lemon and lime juice (in small plastic fruit-shaped bottles found in produce section)
Instant fruit beverage mixes (*Crystal Light*)
Dry dairy beverage mixes (*Nestlé's Quik and Swiss Miss*)
"Ice cream"—*Well's Blue Bunny Health Beat Fat and Sugar Free*

The items on my shopping list are everyday foods found in just about any grocery store in America. But all are as low in fat, sugar, calories, and sodium as I can find—and that still taste good! I can make any recipe in my cookbooks and newsletters as long as I have my cupboards and refrigerator stocked with these items. Whenever I use the last of any one item, I just make sure I pick up another supply the next time I'm at the store.

If your grocer does not stock these items, why not ask if they can be ordered on a trial basis? If the store agrees to do so, be sure to tell your friends to stop by, so that sales are good enough to warrant restocking the new products. Competition for shelf space is fierce, so only products that sell well stay around.

Shopping the Healthy Exchanges Way

Sometimes, as part of a cooking demonstration, I take the group on a field trip to the nearest supermarket. There's no better place to share my discoveries about which healthy products taste best, which are best for you, and which healthy products don't deliver enough taste to include in my recipes.

While I'd certainly enjoy accompanying you to your neighborhood store, we'll have to settle for a field trip *on paper*. I've tasted and tried just about every fat- and sugar-free product on the market, but so many new ones keep coming out all the time, you're going to have to learn to play detective on your own. I've turned label reading into an art, but often the label doesn't tell me everything I need to know.

Sometimes you'll find, as I have, that the product with *no* fat doesn't provide the taste satisfaction you require; other times, a no-fat or low-fat product just doesn't cook up the same way as the original product. And some foods, including even the leanest meats, can't eliminate *all* the fat. That's okay, though—a healthy diet should include anywhere from 15 to 25 percent of total calories from fat on any given day.

Take my word for it—your supermarket is filled with lots of delicious foods that can and should be part of your healthy diet for life. Come, join me as we check it out on the way to the checkout!

First stop, the **salad dressing** aisle. Salad dressing is usually a high-fat food, but there are great alternatives available. Let's look first at the regular Ranch dressing—2 tablespoons have 170 calories and 18 grams of fat—and who can eat just 2 tablespoons? Already, that's about half the fat grams most people should consume in a day. Of course, it's the most flavorful too. Now let's look at the low-fat version. Two tablespoons have 110 calories and 11 grams of fat; they took about half of the fat out, but there's still a lot of sugar there. The fat-free version has 50 calories and zero grams of fat, but they also took most of the flavor out. Here's what you do to get it back: add a tablespoon of fat-free mayonnaise, a few more parsley flakes, and about a half teaspoon of sugar substitute to your two-tablespoon serving. That trick, with the fat-free mayo and sugar substitute, will work with just about any fat-free dressing and give it more of that full-bodied flavor of the high-fat version. Be careful not to add too much sugar substitute—you don't want it to become sickeningly sweet.

I even use Kraft fat-free **mayonnaise** at 10 calories per table-spoon to make scalloped potatoes. The Smart Beat brand is also a good one.

Before I buy anything at the store, I read the label carefully: the total fat plus the saturated fat; I look to see how many calories are in a realistic serving, and I say to myself, would I eat that much—or would I eat more? I look at the sodium and I look at the total carbohydrates. I like to check those ingredients because I'm cooking for diabetics and heart patients, too. And I check the total calories from fat.

Remember that 1 fat gram equals 9 calories, while 1 protein or 1 carbohydrate gram equals 4 calories.

A wonderful new product is I Can't Believe It's Not Butter! spray, with zero calories and zero grams of fat in four squirts. It's great for your air-popped popcorn. As for **light margarine spread**, beware—most of the fat-free brands don't melt on toast, and they don't taste very good either, so I just leave them on the shelf. For the few times I do use a light margarine I tend to buy Smart Beat Ultra, Promise Ultra, or Weight Watchers Light Ultra. The number-one ingredient in them is water. I occasionally use the light margarine in cooking, but I don't really put margarine on my toast anymore. I use apple butter or make a spread with fat-free cream cheese mixed with a little spreadable fruit instead.

So far, Pillsbury hasn't released a reduced-fat **crescent roll**, so you'll only get one crescent roll per serving from me. I usually make eight of the rolls serve twelve by using them for a crust. The house brands may be lower in fat but they're usually not as good flavor-wise—and don't quite cover the pan when you use them to make a crust. If you're going to use crescent rolls with lots of other stuff on top, then a house brand might be fine.

The Pillsbury French Loaf makes a wonderful **pizza crust** and fills a giant jelly roll pan. One-fifth of this package "costs" you only 1 gram of fat (and I don't even let you have that much). Once you use this for your pizza crust, you will never go back to anything else instead. I use it to make calzones too.

I only use Philadelphia Fat Free **cream cheese** because it has the best consistency. I've tried other brands, but I wasn't happy with them. Healthy Choice makes lots of great products, but their cream cheese just doesn't work as well with my recipes.

Let's move to the **cheese** aisle. My preferred brand is Kraft ⅓ less fat shredded cheese. I will not use the fat-free versions because *they don't melt*. I would gladly give up sugar and fat, but I will not give up flavor. This is a happy compromise. I use the reduced-fat version. I use less, and I use it where your eyes "eat" it, on top of the recipe. So you walk away satisfied and with a finished product that's very low in fat. If you want to make grilled-cheese sandwiches for your kids, use the Kraft ⅓ less fat cheese slices, and it'll taste exactly like the one they're used to. The fat-free will not.

Some brands have come out with a fat-free **hot dog**, but the ones we've tasted haven't been very good. So far, among the low-fat brands, I think Healthy Choice tastes the best. Did you know that regular hot dogs have as many as 15 grams of fat?

Dubuque's extra-lean reduced-sodium **ham** tastes wonderful, reduces the sodium as well as the fat, and gives you a larger serving. Don't be fooled by products called turkey ham; they may *not* be lower in fat than a very lean pork product. Here's one label as an example: I checked a brand of turkey ham called Genoa. It gives you a 2-ounce serving for 70 calories and 3½ grams of fat. The Dubuque extra-lean ham, made from pork, gives you a 3-ounce serving for 90 calories, but only 2½ grams of fat. *You get more food and less fat.*

The same can be true of packaged **ground turkey**; if you're not buying *fresh* ground turkey, you may be getting a product with turkey skin and a lot of fat ground up in it. Look to be sure the package is labeled with the fat content; if it isn't, run the other way!

Your best bets in **snack foods** are pretzels, which are always low in fat, as well as the chips from the Guiltless Gourmet, which taste especially good with one of my dips.

Frozen dinners can be expensive and high in sodium, but it's smart to have two or three in the freezer as a backup when your best-laid plans go awry and you need to grab something on the run. It's not a good idea to rely on them too much—what if you can't get to the store to get them, or you're short on cash? The sodium can be high in some of them because they often replace the fat with salt, so do read the labels. Also ask yourself if the serving is enough to satisfy you; for many of us, it's not.

Egg substitute is expensive, and probably not necessary unless you're cooking for someone who has to worry about every bit of cholesterol in his or her diet. If you occasionally have a fried egg or an omelet, *use the real egg.* For cooking, you can usually substitute two egg whites for one whole egg. Most of the time it won't make any difference, but check your recipe carefully.

Frozen pizzas aren't particularly healthy, but used occasion-ally, in moderation, they're okay. Your best bet is to make your own using the Pillsbury French Crust. Take a look at the frozen pizza package of your choice, though, because you may find that plain cheese pizza, which you might think would be the healthiest, might actually have the most fat. Since there's nothing else on there, they have to cover the crust with a heavy layer of high-fat cheese. A veggie pizza generally uses less cheese and more healthy, crunchy vegetables.

Healthy frozen desserts are hard to find except for the Weight Watchers brands. I've always felt that their portions are so small, and for their size still pretty high in fat and sugar. (This is one of the reasons I think I'll be successful marketing my frozen desserts someday.) Keep an eye out for fat-free or very low-fat frozen yogurt or sorbet products. Even Häagen-Dazs, which makes some of the highest-fat-content ice cream, now has a fat-free fruit sorbet pop out that's pretty good. I'm sure there will be more before too long.

You have to be realistic: What are you willing to do, and what are you *not* willing to do? Let's take bread, for example. Some people just have to have the real thing—rye bread with caraway seeds or a whole-wheat version with bits of bran in it.

I prefer to use reduced-calorie **bread** because I like a *real* sandwich. This way, I can have two slices of bread and it counts as only one bread/starch exchange.

Do you love **croutons**? Forget the ones from the grocery store—they're extremely high in fat. Instead, take reduced-calorie bread, toast it, give it a quick spray of I Can't Believe It's Not Butter! spray, and let it dry a bit. Cut the bread in cubes. Then, for an extra-good flavor, put the pieces in a plastic bag with a couple of tablespoons of grated Kraft fat-free Parmesan cheese and shake them up. You might be surprised just how good they are. Here's another product that's really good for croutons—Corn Chex cereal. Sprinkle a few Chex on top of your salad, and I think you'll be pleasantly surprised. I've also found that Rice Chex, crushed up, with parsley flakes and a little bit of Parmesan cheese, makes a great topping for casseroles that you used to put potato chips on.

Salad toppers can make a lot of difference in how content you feel after you've eaten. Some low-fat cheese, some homemade croutons, and even some bacon bits on top of your greens deliver an abundance of tasty satisfaction. I always use the real Hormel **bacon bits** instead of the imitation bacon-flavored bits. I only use a small amount, but you get that real bacon flavor—and less fat, too.

How I Shop

I always keep my kitchen stocked with my basic staples; that way, I can go to the cupboard and create new recipes anytime I'm inspired. I hope you will take the time (and allot the money) to stock your cupboards with items from the staples list, so you can enjoy developing your own healthy versions of family favorites without making extra trips to the market.

I'm always on the lookout for new products sitting on the grocery shelf. When I spot something I haven't seen before, I'll usually grab it, glance at the front, then turn it around and read the label carefully. I call it looking at the promises (the "come-on" on the front of the package) and then at the warranty (the ingredients list and the label on the back).

If it looks as good on the back as it does on the front, I'll say okay and either create a recipe on the spot or take it home for when I do think of something to do with it. Picking up a new product is just about the only time I buy something not on my list.

The items on my shopping list are normal, everyday foods, but as low-fat and low-sugar (*while still tasting good*) as I can find. I can make any recipe in this book as long as these staples are on my shelves. After using these products for a couple of weeks, you will find it becomes routine to have them on hand. And I promise you, I really don't spend any more at the store now than I did a few years ago when I told myself I couldn't afford some of these items. Back then, of course, plenty of unhealthy, high-priced snacks I really didn't need somehow made the magic leap from the grocery shelves into my cart. Who was I kidding?

Yes, you often have to pay a little more for fat-free or low-fat products, including meats. But since I frequently use a half pound of meat to serve four to six people, your cost per serving will be much lower.

Try adding up what you were spending before on chips and cookies, premium brand ice cream and fatty cuts of meat, and you'll soon see that we've *streamlined* your shopping cart—and taken the weight off your pocketbook as well as your hips!

Remember, your good health is *your* business—but it's big business, too. Write to the manufacturers of products you and your family enjoy but feel are just too high in fat, sugar, or sodium to be part of your new healthy lifestyle. Companies are spending millions of dollars to respond to consumers' concerns about food products, and I bet that in the next few years, you'll discover fat-free and low-fat versions of nearly every product piled high on your supermarket shelves!

The Healthy Exchanges Kitchen

You might be surprised to discover I still don't have a massive test kitchen stocked with every modern appliance and handy gadget ever made. The tiny galley kitchen where I first launched Healthy Exchanges has room for only one person at a time in it, but that never stopped me from feeling the sky's the limit when it comes to seeking out great healthy taste!

Because storage is at such a premium in my kitchen, I don't waste space with equipment I don't really need. Here's a list of what I consider worth having. If you notice serious gaps in your equipment, you can probably find most of what you need at a local discount store or garage sale. If your kitchen is equipped with more sophisticated appliances, don't feel guilty about using them. Enjoy every appliance you can find room for or that you can afford. Just be assured that healthy, quick, and delicious food can be prepared with the "basics."

A Healthy Exchanges Kitchen Equipment List

Good-quality nonstick skillets (medium, large)
Good-quality saucepans (small, medium, large)
Glass mixing bowls (small, medium, large)
Glass measures (1-cup, 2-cup, 4-cup, 8-cup)
Sharp knives (paring, chef, butcher)
Rubber spatulas
Wire whisks
Measuring spoons
Large mixing spoons
Egg separator
Covered jar
Vegetable parer
Grater
Potato masher
Electric mixer
Electric blender
Electric skillet
Cooking timer
Slow cooker
Air popper for popcorn
4-inch round custard dishes
Glass pie plates
8-by-8-inch glass baking dishes
Cake pans (9-by-9, 9-by-13-inch)
$10\frac{3}{4}$-by-7-by-$1\frac{1}{2}$-inch biscuit pan
Cookie sheets (good nonstick ones)
Jelly roll pan
Muffin tins
5-by-9-inch bread pan
Plastic colander
Cutting board
Pie wedge server
Square-shaped server

Can opener (I prefer manual)
Rolling pin
Kitchen scales (unless you *always* use my recipes)
Wire racks for cooling baked goods
Electric toaster oven (to conserve energy for those times
when only one item is being baked or for a recipe that
calls for a short baking time)

How to Read a Healthy Exchanges Recipe

The Healthy Exchanges Nutritional Analysis

Before using these recipes, you may wish to consult your physician or health-care provider to be sure they are appropriate for you. The information in this book is not intended to take the place of any medical advice. It reflects my experiences, studies, research, and opinions regarding healthy eating.

Each recipe includes nutritional information calculated in three ways:

Healthy Exchanges Weight Loss Choices or Exchanges
Calories, fiber, and fat grams
Diabetic exchanges

In every Healthy Exchanges recipe, the diabetic exchanges have been calculated by a registered dietitian. All the other calculations were done by computer, using the Food Processor II software. When the ingredient listing gives more than one choice, the first ingredient listed is the one used in the recipe analysis. Due to inevitable variations in the ingredients you choose to use, the nutritional values should be considered approximate.

The annotation "(limited)" following Protein counts in some

recipes indicates that consumption of whole eggs should be limited to four per week.

Please note the following symbols:

☆   This star means read the recipe's directions carefully for special instructions about **division** of ingredients.

❋   This symbol indicates **FREEZES WELL**.

A Few Cooking Terms to Ease the Way

Everyone can learn to cook *The Healthy Exchanges Way*. It's simple, it's quick, and the results are delicious! If you've tended to avoid the kitchen because you find recipe instructions confusing or complicated, I hope I can help you feel more confident. I'm not offering a full cooking course here, just some terms I use often that I know you'll want to understand.

Bake:	To cook food in the oven; sometimes called roasting
Beat:	To mix very fast with a spoon, wire whisk, or electric mixer
Blend:	To mix two or more ingredients together thoroughly so that the mixture is smooth
Boil:	To cook in liquid until bubbles form
Brown:	To cook at low to medium-low heat until ingredients turn brown
Chop:	To cut food into small pieces with a knife, blender, or food processor
Cool:	To let stand at room temperature until food is no longer hot to the touch
Combine:	To mix ingredients together with a spoon

Dice:	To chop into small, even-sized pieces
Drain:	To pour off liquid; sometimes you will need to re-serve the liquid to use in the recipe, so please read carefully
Drizzle:	To sprinkle drops of liquid (for example, chocolate syrup) lightly over top of food
Fold in:	To combine delicate ingredients with other foods by using a gentle, circular motion. Example: adding Cool Whip Lite to an already stirred-up bowl of pudding
Preheat:	To heat your oven to the desired temperature, usually about ten minutes before you put your food in to bake
Sauté:	To cook in a skillet or frying pan until food is soft
Simmer:	To cook in a small amount of liquid over low heat; this lets the flavors blend without too much liquid evaporating
Whisk:	To beat with a wire whisk until mixture is well mixed; don't worry about finesse here, just use some elbow grease!

How to Measure

I try to make it as easy as possible by providing more than one measurement for many ingredients in my recipes—both the weight in ounces and the amount measured by a measuring cup, for example. Just remember:

- You measure **solids** (flour, Cool Whip Lite, yogurt, macaroni, nonfat dry milk powder) in your set of separate measuring cups (¼, ⅓, ½, 1 cup)
- You measure **liquids** (Diet Mountain Dew, water, tomato juice) in the clear glass or plastic measuring cups that mea-

sure ounces, cups, and pints. Set the cup on a level surface and pour the liquid into it, or you may get too much.

- You can use your measuring spoon set for liquids or solids. **Note:** Don't pour a liquid like an extract into a measuring spoon held over the bowl and run the risk of overpouring; instead, do it over the sink.

Here are a few handy equivalents:

3 teaspoons	equal	1 tablespoon
4 tablespoons	equal	¼ cup
5⅓ tablespoons	equal	⅓ cup
8 tablespoons	equal	½ cup
10⅔ tablespoons	equal	⅔ cup
12 tablespoons	equal	¾ cup
16 tablespoons	equal	1 cup
2 cups	equal	1 pint
4 cups	equal	1 quart
8 ounces liquid	equal	1 fluid cup

That's it. Now, ready, set, cook!

Party Starters

Strike up the band and let the party begin! To launch your special gathering with real pizazz, why not invite your guests to partake of one or more of my festive appetizers and soups? They're quick to fix, fill your home with irresistibly good aromas, and put everyone in a great mood for the evening!

If you're looking to warm up after an evening of carol singing, I've got cozy soups so full of delectable ingredients they're almost as thick as stews. You'll also find spicy, flavorful dips as well as fun "finger food" and fresh-baked breads and muffins.

If you're celebrating a birthday or inviting distant relatives for a family reunion, you're bound to find a special first course among these tried-and-true favorites that's just right for your special occasion.

Don't be surprised if everyone crowds into the kitchen to see what's cooking—often the best conversations take place in the heart of the house!

Party Starters

Salsa Party Dip	58
Hawaiian Mint Dip	58
Chocolate Caribbean Fruit Dip	59
Dill Pickle Rings	60
Veggie Salad Rye Rounds	61
Ham and Cheese Pinwheels	62
Chinese Chicken Soup	63
Thai Pork Soup	64
Italian Beef and Noodle Soup	65
Carrot Cake Muffins	66
Apple Orchard Muffins	68
Cinnamon Cream Rolls	70
Cinnamon-Apple Corn Bread	71
Banana Pecan Bread	72
Fresh Strawberry Punch	73
Ham and Pea Salad Stuffed Tomatoes	74
Tuna Garden Wedges	75
Salad Bar Pizza	76
Party Pizza Bites	77

Salsa Party Dip

This spicy concoction tastes so fresh, your guests will scoop it up with gusto! Experiment until you decide how hot you like it, and try different salsa brands to find the one that stirs up the smoothest.

○ Serves 8 (⅓ cup each)

> 1 (8-ounce) package Philadelphia fat-free cream cheese
> ⅓ cup Kraft fat-free mayonnaise
> 1 cup chunky salsa (mild, medium, or hot)
> 1 teaspoon dried parsley flakes

In a medium bowl, stir cream cheese with a spoon until soft. Add mayonnaise. Mix well to combine. Blend in salsa and parsley flakes. Refrigerate for at least 30 minutes. Gently stir again just before serving.

HINT: Good with fresh veggies or crackers.

Each serving equals:

HE: ½ Protein • ¼ Vegetable • 7 Optional Calories

28 Calories • 0 gm Fat • 4 gm Protein •
3 gm Carbohydrate • 349 mg Sodium • 0 gm Fiber

DIABETIC: ½ Meat

Hawaiian Mint Dip

If you've never tried a dip flavored with fruit and made even more special with the addition of a fresh herb like mint, give this one a whirl. It's so light and lush, you'll imagine a fragrant island breeze is just around the corner! ○ Serves 8 (3 tablespoons each)

> 1 (8-ounce) package Philadelphia fat-free cream cheese
> 1 cup (one 8-ounce can) crushed pineapple, packed in fruit juice,
>   drained
> 2 tablespoons Kraft fat-free mayonnaise
> ½ teaspoon mint extract or 2 tablespoons chopped fresh mint

In a medium bowl, stir cream cheese with a spoon until soft. Add pineapple and mayonnaise. Mix well to combine. Stir in mint. Refrigerate for at least 30 minutes. Gently stir again just before serving.

Each serving equals:

HE: ½ Protein • ¼ Fruit • 2 Optional Calories

40 Calories • 0 gm Fat • 4 gm Protein •
6 gm Carbohydrate • 196 mg Sodium • 0 gm Fiber

DIABETIC: ½ Meat • ½ Fruit

Chocolate Caribbean Fruit Dip

Here's something your guests may not expect—a sweet dip! But I bet they'll be more than pleased when you offer this delectable mixture flavored with chocolate and rum. This dip is truly luscious with everything from apple and pear slices to chunks of fresh melon.

◐ Serves 8 (scant ⅓ cup)

2 (8-ounce) packages Philadelphia fat-free cream cheese
¼ cup Nestlé Quik sugar-free chocolate mix
¼ cup hot coffee
2 teaspoons coconut extract
2 teaspoons rum extract
2 tablespoons Sugar Twin or Sprinkle Sweet
½ cup Cool Whip Lite

In a medium bowl, stir cream cheese with a spoon until soft. Add Nestlé Quik, coffee, coconut extract, rum extract, and Sugar Twin. Mix well to combine. Blend in Cool Whip Lite. Refrigerate for at least 30 minutes. Gently stir again just before serving.

Each serving equals:

HE: 1 Protein • ¼ Slider • 4 Optional Calories

61 Calories • 1 gm Fat • 8 gm Protein •
6 gm Carbohydrate • 352 mg Sodium • 0 gm Fiber

DIABETIC: 1 Meat • ½ Starch *or* Carbohydrate

Dill Pickle Rings

If you're a pickle lover and in the market for a fun new hors d'oeuvre, this might just fit the bill! It's got crunch, it's got meaty goodness that tastes like a special treat, and it's creamy too. I like it best with dill pickles, but you could try this with other types of pickled vegetables like carrots or green beans.

◐ Serves 8 (8 slices each)

8 dill pickles
1 (8-ounce) package Philadelphia fat-free cream cheese
1 teaspoon dried parsley flakes
2 (2.5-ounce) packages Carl Buddig lean sliced ham or corned beef

Dry dill pickles with a paper towel. In a small bowl, stir cream cheese with a spoon until soft. Stir in parsley flakes. Frost each pickle with 2 tablespoons cream cheese mixture. Divide meat slices into 8 bundles. Wrap a meat bundle around each pickle. Cover and refrigerate for at least 30 minutes. Slice each wrapped pickle into 8 slices, using a very sharp knife. Cover and refrigerate at least 15 minutes.

Each serving equals:

HE: 1 Protein • 1 Vegetable • 7 Optional Calories

54 Calories • 2 gm Fat • 7 gm Protein •
2 gm Carbohydrate • 393 mg Sodium • 0 gm Fiber

DIABETIC: 1 Meat • 1 Vegetable

Veggie Salad Rye Rounds

These colorful bites are easy to serve and eat, and the melange of fresh vegetable chunks makes a rainbow on your buffet table. If you've never used lemon pepper, let me encourage you to invest in a bottle now. It's a sensational addition to all kinds of dishes, especially vegetables!   ○   Serves 8

1 (8-ounce) package Philadelphia fat-free cream cheese
2 tablespoons dill pickle relish
⅛ teaspoon lemon pepper
¼ cup Kraft fat-free mayonnaise
¼ cup chopped green bell pepper
½ cup unpeeled chopped cucumbers
½ cup finely chopped fresh tomatoes
¼ cup finely chopped celery
¼ cup chopped onion
2 tablespoons snipped fresh parsley
32 rye bread rounds or squares

In a large bowl, stir cream cheese with a spoon until soft. Add dill pickle relish, lemon pepper, mayonnaise, green pepper, cucumbers, tomatoes, celery, onion, and parsley. Mix gently to combine. Evenly spoon about 1 full tablespoon mixture on each round. Cover and refrigerate for at least 30 minutes.

HINT: Pumpernickel bread rounds are also good.

Each serving equals:

HE: 1 Bread • ½ Vegetable • ½ Protein •
5 Optional Calories

150 Calories • 2 gm Fat • 8 gm Protein •
25 gm Carbohydrate • 507 mg Sodium • 0 gm Fiber

DIABETIC: 1 Starch • 1 Meat

Ham and Cheese Pinwheels

Here's a wonderfully old-fashioned party treat made healthier with the addition of low-fat ingredients. You'll love how pretty these look on the plate—but beware, they won't last long! Everyone will grab them while they're still a little hot. ○ Serves 8 (2 each)

1 (8-ounce) can Pillsbury refrigerated crescent rolls
1 (2.5-ounce) package Carl Buddig lean sliced ham
4 (¾-ounce) slices Kraft reduced-fat American cheese

Preheat oven to 375 degrees. Spray a cookie sheet with butter-flavored cooking spray. Separate dough into 4 rectangles. Divide ham slices into 4 bundles. Place a bundle of ham and 1 slice of cheese on each rectangle. Roll each rectangle as for cinnamon rolls. Cut each into 4 pieces. Place pieces on prepared cookie sheet. Bake for 8 to 10 minutes or until golden brown. Remove from oven and lightly spray tops with butter-flavored cooking spray. Place cookie sheet on a wire rack and let set for 5 minutes.

Each serving equals:

HE: 1 Bread • ¾ Protein • 4 Optional Calories

123 Calories • 7 gm Fat • 4 gm Protein •
11 gm Carbohydrate • 340 mg Sodium • 0 gm Fiber

DIABETIC: 1 Starch • ½ Meat • ½ Fat

Chinese Chicken Soup

This restaurant classic combines the soothing warmth of old-time chicken soup flavor with those delectable ingredients that add the taste and texture of the mysterious East. On a rainy night when all you want is to feel cozy, this is a great buffet choice.

○ Serves 8 (1¼ cups)

> 4 cups (two 16-ounce cans) Healthy Request Chicken Broth
> 2 cups water
> 2 cups sliced celery
> 1 cup chopped onion
> ¼ teaspoon dried minced garlic
> 2 cups (10 ounces) diced cooked chicken breast
> 1 cup (two 2.5-ounce jars) sliced mushrooms, drained
> 1 tablespoon reduced-sodium soy sauce
> 1⅓ cups (4 ounces) uncooked instant rice
> 2 (6-ounce) packages frozen snow peas
> 1 cup (one 8-ounce can) sliced water chestnuts, drained

In a large saucepan, combine chicken broth, water, celery, onion, and garlic. Bring mixture to a boil. Add chicken, mushrooms, and soy sauce. Mix well to combine. Stir in rice, snow peas, and water chestnuts. Lower heat and simmer for 15 minutes or until vegetables and rice are tender, stirring occasionally.

HINT: If you don't have leftovers, purchase a chunk of cooked chicken breast from your local deli.

Each serving equals:

HE: 1½ Vegetable • 1¼ Protein • ¾ Bread • 8 Optional Calories

137 Calories • 1 gm Fat • 15 gm Protein • 17 gm Carbohydrate • 386 mg Sodium • 3 gm Fiber

DIABETIC: 1 Starch • 1 Vegetable • 1 Meat

Thai Pork Soup

When you spot peanut butter in the list of ingredients here, you may be surprised, but you'll be delighted by the fragrant aroma of this meaty, tangy soup inspired by the cuisine of Thailand. Because it uses the best in prepared ingredients, this dish can be ready in a real hurry!   ●   Serves 8 (1½ cups)

> 3 cups V-8 reduced-sodium vegetable juice
> 1¾ cups (one 14½-ounce can) Swanson Beef Broth
> 1¾ cups water
> 8 cups purchased stir-fry vegetables
> 2 full cups (12 ounces) diced cooked lean roast pork
> ¼ teaspoon black pepper
> ¼ cup reduced-sodium soy sauce
> 1⅓ cups (4 ounces) uncooked instant rice
> ¼ cup Peter Pan reduced-fat peanut butter

In a large saucepan, combine vegetable juice, beef broth, and water. Bring mixture to a boil. Add vegetables, pork, and black pepper. Mix well to combine. Cook just until vegetables are tender, about 8 minutes, stirring occasionally. Stir in soy sauce, instant rice, and peanut butter. Lower heat, cover, and simmer for 10 minutes or until rice is tender.

HINT: If you don't have leftovers, purchase a chunk of cooked roast pork from your local deli.

Each serving equals:

HE: 2¾ Vegetable • 2 Protein • ½ Bread • ½ Fat • 4 Optional Calories

---

250 Calories • 6 gm Fat • 18 gm Protein • 31 gm Carbohydrate • 826 mg Sodium • 5 gm Fiber

---

DIABETIC: 3 Vegetable • 2 Meat • 1 Starch

Italian Beef and Noodle Soup

You may not always think of Italy when you think of soup—it's more famous for pasta, after all. But this blend of hearty beef broth with Parmesan cheese and Italian seasoning will have you dreaming of a Roman holiday sometime soon!

☻ Serves 8 (1½ cups)

> 16 ounces ground 90% lean turkey or beef
> ½ cup chopped onion
> 1¾ cups (one 15-ounce can) Swanson Beef Broth
> 2 cups water
> 3½ cups (two 14½-ounce cans) stewed tomatoes, undrained
> 2 teaspoons Italian seasoning
> 2⅔ cups (4.5 ounces) uncooked noodles
> ⅛ teaspoon black pepper
> ½ cup (1½ ounces) grated Kraft fat-free Parmesan cheese

In a large saucepan sprayed with olive oil–flavored cooking spray, brown meat and onion. Add beef broth, water, undrained stewed tomatoes, and Italian seasoning. Mix well to combine. Stir in uncooked noodles and black pepper. Lower heat and simmer for 25 to 30 minutes, stirring occasionally. When serving, sprinkle 1 tablespoon Parmesan cheese over top of each bowl.

Each serving equals:

HE: 1¾ Protein • 1 Vegetable • ¾ Bread •
4 Optional Calories

237 Calories • 8 gm Fat • 18 gm Protein •
23 gm Carbohydrate • 616 mg Sodium • 1 gm Fiber

DIABETIC: 2 Meat • 1 Vegetable • 1 Starch

Carrot Cake Muffins

The addition of pumpkin pie spice to this easy carrot cake recipe will make your guests' mouth water when you serve these at a casual weekend brunch! You'll be delighted to see how well applesauce works in place of shortening, and how moist these muffins turn out. They're also delicious the next day, so hope for leftovers!

● Serves 8

1½ cups all-purpose flour

1 (4-serving) package JELL-O sugar-free instant vanilla pudding mix

¼ cup Sugar Twin or Sprinkle Sweet

1 teaspoon baking powder

1 teaspoon baking soda

1 teaspoon pumpkin pie spice

1 cup grated carrots

½ cup raisins

¼ cup (1 ounce) chopped walnuts

1 cup (one 8-ounce can) crushed pineapple, packed in fruit juice, undrained

2 tablespoons vegetable oil

1 teaspoon vanilla extract

1 egg or equivalent in egg substitute

¼ cup skim milk

Preheat oven to 350 degrees. Spray 8 wells of a 12-hole muffin pan with butter-flavored cooking spray or line with paper liners. In a large bowl, combine flour, dry pudding mix, Sugar Twin, baking powder, baking soda, and pumpkin pie spice. Add carrots, raisins, and walnuts. Mix well to combine. In a small bowl, combine undrained pineapple, vegetable oil, vanilla extract, egg, and skim milk. Add pineapple mixture to flour mixture. Mix gently just to combine. Fill prepared muffin wells ¾ full. Bake for 20 to 22 minutes or until a toothpick inserted in center comes out clean. Place muffin pan on a wire rack and let set for 5 minutes. Remove muffins from pan and continue cooling on wire rack.

HINT: Fill unused muffin wells with water. It protects the muffin tin and ensures even baking.

Each serving equals:

HE: 1 Bread • 1 Fat • ¾ Fruit • ¼ Vegetable • ¼ Protein • 18 Optional Calories

---

214 Calories • 6 gm Fat • 4 gm Protein • 36 gm Carbohydrate • 404 mg Sodium • 2 gm Fiber

---

DIABETIC: 1 Starch • 1 Fat • 1 Fruit *or* 1 Carbohydrate • 1 Fat

Apple Orchard Muffins

If you've got the time and the place to go apple picking as a family, you're bound to come home with more apples than you could ever eat. But even if you simply buy a bunch of lush red fruit at the grocery store, you'll enjoy whipping up a batch of these sweet treats. A healthy apple muffin can help "keep the doctor away" too!

⊙ Serves 8

⅔ cup Carnation Nonfat Dry Milk Powder

¾ cup water

2 teaspoons white vinegar

1½ cups all-purpose flour

1 teaspoon baking powder

½ teaspoon baking soda

1½ teaspoons apple pie spice

¼ cup Sugar Twin or Sprinkle Sweet

1 cup (2 small) cored, unpeeled, and finely diced cooking apples

2 tablespoons vegetable oil

1 egg, slightly beaten, or equivalent in egg substitute

Preheat oven to 400 degrees. In a small bowl, combine dry milk powder, water, and vinegar. Set aside. Spray 8 wells of a 12-hole muffin pan with butter-flavored cooking spray or line with paper liners. In a large bowl, combine flour, baking powder, baking soda, apple pie spice, and Sugar Twin. Stir in apples. Add vegetable oil and egg to milk mixture. Mix well to combine. Stir milk mixture into flour mixture, just to combine. Fill prepared muffin wells ¾ full. Bake for 20 to 22 minutes or until a toothpick inserted in center comes out clean. Place muffin pan on a wire rack and let set for 5 minutes. Remove muffins from pan and continue cooling on wire rack.

HINT: Fill unused muffin wells with water. It protects the muffin tin and ensures even baking.

Each serving equals:

HE: 1 Bread • ¾ Fat • ¼ Fruit • ¼ Skim Milk •
10 Optional Calories

152 Calories • 4 gm Fat • 5 gm Protein •
24 gm Carbohydrate • 180 mg Sodium • 1 gm Fiber

DIABETIC: 1 Starch • 1 Fat • ½ Fruit

Cinnamon Cream Rolls

Is there a better scent on earth than that of cinnamon rolls baking? From coast to coast, cafes have opened up selling just this beloved taste treat. Now you can make a wonderfully healthy version at home in very little time, and the fragrance of cinnamon and raisins will perfume your kitchen for hours.   ❂ Serves 8 (2 each)

> 1 (8-ounce) can Pillsbury refrigerated crescent rolls
> ½ cup (4 ounces) Philadelphia fat-free cream cheese
> 1 teaspoon ground cinnamon
> 2 tablespoons Sugar Twin or Sprinkle Sweet
> ¼ cup raisins

Preheat oven to 400 degrees. Spray a cookie sheet with butter-flavored cooking spray. Separate dough into 4 rectangles. In a small bowl, stir cream cheese with a spoon until soft. Spread 2 table-spoons softened cream cheese over each rectangle. In a small bowl, combine cinnamon and Sugar Twin. Evenly sprinkle cinnamon mixture over cream cheese. Sprinkle 1 tablespoon raisins over top of each rectangle. Roll each rectangle as for cinnamon rolls. Cut each into 4 pieces. Place pieces on prepared cookie sheet. Lightly spray tops with butter-flavored cooking spray. Bake for 7 to 8 minutes or until golden brown. Remove from oven and lightly spray again. Remove rolls from pan and place on a wire rack and cool for at least 5 minutes. Good warm or cold.

Each serving equals:

HE: 1 Bread • ¼ Protein • ¼ Fruit • 2 Optional Calories

125 Calories • 5 gm Fat • 4 gm Protein •
16 gm Carbohydrate • 315 mg Sodium • 0 gm Fiber

DIABETIC: 1 Starch • 1 Fat

Cinnamon-Apple Corn Bread

Most corn bread recipes tend to be more tangy than sweet, with added ingredients like colorful peppers or bright yellow corn. I love the taste of corn bread but thought a sweeter version would be great for a lazy breakfast with relatives during a family reunion. The cinnamon in the apple mix is a little unexpected with corn bread, but tastes extra good! ☉ Serves 8

1 cup yellow cornmeal
¾ cup all-purpose flour
¼ cup Sugar Twin or
   Sprinkle Sweet
2 teaspoons baking powder
1 teaspoon apple pie spice
¼ cup (1 ounce) chopped
   walnuts

1 cup unsweetened
   applesauce
1 egg or equivalent in egg
   substitute
2 tablespoons vegetable oil
½ cup skim milk

Preheat oven to 350 degrees. Spray an 8-by-8-inch baking dish with butter-flavored cooking spray. In a large bowl, combine cornmeal, flour, Sugar Twin, baking powder, apple pie spice, and walnuts. In a small bowl, combine applesauce, egg, vegetable oil, and skim milk. Add applesauce mixture to cornmeal mixture. Mix gently just until moistened. Spread mixture into prepared baking dish. Bake for 16 to 20 minutes or until a toothpick inserted in center comes out clean. Place baking dish on a wire rack and let set for at least 5 minutes. Cut into 8 servings.

HINT: Good warm or cold. Also good served with Cary's Sugar Free Maple Syrup.

Each serving equals:
   HE: 1½ Bread • 1 Fat • ¼ Protein • ¼ Fruit •
   9 Optional Calories

   173 Calories • 5 gm Fat • 4 gm Protein •
   28 gm Carbohydrate • 110 mg Sodium • 2 gm Fiber

   DIABETIC: 2 Starch • 1 Fat

Banana Pecan Bread

Every cook should have a great recipe for banana bread, as it's one of the most popular quick breads there is. This one will bake up moist and so sweetly scented, you'll wish your kitchen always smelled this yummy! The crunch of the pecans adds texture and flavor to this beloved classic.

⊙ Serves 8 (1 thick or 2 thin slices)

1½ cups all-purpose flour

1 (4-serving) package JELL-O sugar-free instant banana pudding mix

1 teaspoon baking soda

1 teaspoon baking powder

1 teaspoon pumpkin pie spice

⅓ cup (1½ ounces) chopped pecans

1⅓ cups (2 medium) mashed ripe bananas

2 eggs or equivalent in egg substitute

½ cup unsweetened applesauce

⅓ cup unsweetened apple juice

Preheat oven to 350 degrees. Spray a 9-by-5-inch loaf pan with butter-flavored cooking spray. In a medium bowl, combine flour, dry pudding mix, baking soda, baking powder, pumpkin pie spice, and pecans. In a small bowl, combine mashed bananas, eggs, applesauce, and apple juice. Add banana mixture to flour mixture. Mix gently to combine. Pour mixture into prepared loaf pan. Bake for 1 hour or until a toothpick inserted in center comes out clean. Place pan on a wire rack and let set for 5 minutes. Remove bread from pan and continue cooling on wire rack. Cut into 8 thick or 16 thin slices.

Each serving equals:

HE: 1 Bread • ¾ Fat • ⅔ Fruit • ¼ Protein (limited) •
13 Optional Calories

205 Calories • 5 gm Fat • 5 gm Protein •
35 gm Carbohydrate • 406 mg Sodium • 2 gm Fiber

DIABETIC: 1 Starch • 1 Fat • 1 Fruit *or*
2 Carbohydrate • 1 Fat

Fresh Strawberry Punch

This is an irresistibly scrumptious party drink to serve during those
months (like May!) when strawberries are at their ripest and least
expensive! What a luscious color this combination of fruit punch,
lemony soda, and fresh strawberries produces. Try floating a few
berry slices on top as a garnish.   ☻   Serves 8 (1 cup)

1 tub Crystal Light Fruit Punch
3 cups Diet Mountain Dew
4 cups water
2 cups chopped fresh strawberries

In a large pitcher, combine fruit punch powder, Diet Mountain
Dew, and water. Pour 2 cups of the mixture into a blender container. Add chopped strawberries. Cover and blend on HIGH for
30 seconds or until strawberries are liquefied. Pour blended strawberry mixture into remaining punch mixture. Mix well to blend.
Serve over ice.

Each serving equals:

HE: ¼ Fruit • 5 Optional Calories

4 Calories • 0 gm Fat • 0 gm Protein •
1 gm Carbohydrate • 13 mg Sodium • 0 gm Fiber

DIABETIC: 1 Free Food

Ham and Pea Salad Stuffed Tomatoes

I took a lot of favorite flavors and blended them in this easy-to-serve party dish. Served on a white plate, this dish will immediately attract attention with its pretty collage of colors.

● Serves 8

> ½ cup Kraft fat-free mayonnaise
> 2 teaspoons prepared mustard
> ⅛ teaspoon black pepper
> 2 cups frozen peas, thawed
> 2 full cups (12 ounces) diced Dubuque 97% fat-free ham or any extra-lean ham
> 2 teaspoons dried onion flakes
> 8 ripe (medium-sized) tomatoes
> Lettuce leaves

In a large bowl, combine mayonnaise, mustard, and black pepper. Add peas, ham, and onion flakes. Cover and refrigerate for at least 30 minutes. Just before serving, slice top off tomatoes and scoop out center pulp and seeds. Spoon about ½ cup pea-ham salad into each tomato. Serve on lettuce leaves.

HINT: Thaw peas by placing in a colander and rinsing under hot water for one minute.

Each serving equals:

HE: 1 Protein • 1 Vegetable • ½ Bread • 10 Optional Calories

118 Calories • 2 gm Fat • 10 gm Protein • 15 gm Carbohydrate • 496 mg Sodium • 3 gm Fiber

DIABETIC: 1 Meat • 1 Vegetable • ½ Starch

Tuna Garden Wedges

If you're looking for something different to do with tuna, here's a simple but very attractive dish brimming with tangy flavor. Isn't it great to have healthy prepared dough mixes that bake up so flaky, your guests will be sure you're covered with flour! ● Serves 8

1 (8-ounce) can Pillsbury refrigerated crescent rolls
1 (8-ounce) package Philadelphia fat-free cream cheese
½ cup Kraft fat-free mayonnaise
2 teaspoons prepared horseradish
1 (12-ounce) can white tuna, packed in water, drained and
    flaked
¼ cup sliced green onion
1 teaspoon dried parsley flakes
¾ cup finely chopped celery
1 cup shredded carrots

Preheat oven to 425 degrees. Spray a rimmed 9-by-13-inch cookie sheet with butter-flavored cooking spray. Gently pat rolls into prepared pan being sure to seal perforations. Bake for 6 to 8 minutes or until light golden brown. Place cookie sheet on a wire rack and allow to cool. In a medium bowl, stir cream cheese with a spoon until soft. Blend in mayonnaise and horseradish. Add tuna, green onion, and parsley flakes. Mix well to combine. Stir in celery and carrots. Spread mixture evenly over cooled crust. Refrigerate for at least 1 hour. Cut into 8 servings.

HINT: DO NOT use inexpensive rolls. They don't cover the pan properly.

Each serving equals:
    HE: 1¼ Protein • 1 Bread • ½ Vegetable •
    10 Optional Calories

    186 Calories • 6 gm Fat • 16 gm Protein •
    17 gm Carbohydrate • 641 mg Sodium • 1 gm Fiber

    DIABETIC: 1½ Meat • 1 Starch • 1 Fat

Salad Bar Pizza

Individual wedges of veggie pizza made extra tangy with a creamy dressing? That sounds like a perfect choice for a festive buffet, and your guests will love you for serving up such good-tasting treats that make healthy choices a breeze!   ○ Serves 8 (2 pieces)

1 (8-ounce) can Pillsbury refrigerated crescent rolls
1 (8-ounce) package Philadelphia fat-free cream cheese
⅓ cup Kraft fat-free mayonnaise
¼ cup Kraft Fat Free Ranch Dressing
¾ cup chopped fresh cauliflower
¾ cup chopped fresh broccoli
½ cup shredded carrots
¼ cup diced onion
½ cup diced green bell pepper
¾ cup sliced fresh mushrooms
½ cup sliced radishes
¾ cup (3 ounces) shredded Kraft reduced-fat Cheddar cheese

Preheat oven to 425 degrees. Spray a rimmed 9-by-13-inch cookie sheet with olive oil–flavored cooking spray. Gently pat rolls into prepared pan, being sure to seal perforations. Bake for 6 to 7 minutes or until light golden brown. Place cookie sheet on a wire rack and allow to cool. In a small bowl, stir cream cheese with a spoon until soft. Add mayonnaise and Ranch dressing. Mix well to combine. Evenly spread mixture over cooled crust. In a large bowl, combine cauliflower, broccoli, carrots, onion, green pepper, mushrooms, and radishes. Sprinkle vegetables evenly over cream cheese mixture. Sprinkle Cheddar cheese evenly over top. Refrigerate for at least 1 hour. Cut into 16 pieces.

HINTS: 1.   If you don't care for any of these fresh veggies, substitute ones you like.

2.   DO NOT use inexpensive rolls. They don't cover the pan properly.

Each serving equals:

HE: 1 Bread • 1 Vegetable • 1 Protein •
19 Optional Calories

161 Calories • 7 gm Fat • 8 gm Protein •
17 gm Carbohydrate • 551 mg Sodium • 2 gm Fiber

DIABETIC: 1 Starch • 1 Meat • ½ Vegetable • ½ Fat

Party Pizza Bites

When you're organizing a party for teens or a quick supper before a football game, these individual homemade pizzas are wonderfully quick and easy to whip up. If you're feeling energetic, you could add a bit of green pepper or mushroom to the toppings.

☻ Serves 8 (4 pieces)

> 1 cup (one 8-ounce can) Hunt's Tomato Sauce
> 1 teaspoon Italian seasoning
> 4 English muffins, halved
> ¾ cup (3 ounces) shredded Kraft reduced-fat mozzarella cheese
> ¾ cup (3 ounces) shredded Kraft reduced-fat Cheddar cheese

Preheat oven to 350 degrees. Spray a large cookie sheet with olive oil–flavored cooking spray. In a small bowl, combine tomato sauce and Italian seasoning. Spoon about 1 tablespoon sauce mixture over each muffin half. Evenly sprinkle mozzarella and Cheddar cheese over top. Place muffin halves on prepared cookie sheet. Bake for 10 minutes. Cut each muffin into 4 pieces. Serve hot.

Each serving equals:

HE: 1 Bread • 1 Protein • ½ Vegetable

123 Calories • 3 gm Fat • 8 gm Protein •
16 gm Carbohydrate • 475 mg Sodium • 1 gm Fiber

DIABETIC: 1 Starch • 1 Meat

Sensational Sides

In our family, our party just isn't a party if it doesn't include those beloved foods flavored with so many wonderful memories—tangy potato salads, creamy vegetable dishes, colorful fresh combos that seem to bring the garden indoors!

Once you've selected the perfect entrees for your festive affair, it's time to "hire" the co-stars, those scrumptious side dishes that fill the plate with luscious possibilities and savory pleasures. Try to create a melange of colors and textures that complement the recipes you've chosen to feature in the center of the table; these "supporting performers" are an important ingredient in designing a delicious menu.

I like to include one of my sweet salads each time I entertain—it's a midwestern tradition that appeals to me, and that I've shared with people from every part of the country. You'll find an abundance of ideas in this section, each one a taste treat worthy of your family and friends.

Sensational Sides

Molded Garden Salad	81
Gazpacho Salad	82
Catalina Isle Salad	83
Grande Bean and Carrot Toss	84
Mustard Cucumber Salad	85
Rainbow Tossed Salad	86
Dill Pickle–Cheese Salad Toss	87
French Copper Pennies	88
Blue Cheese Mushroom Salad	89
Colorful Cauliflower Buffet Salad	90
Carrot-Pineapple Toss	91
Cherry Waldorf Salad	92
Apricot Salad	93
Peachy Keen Salad	94
Fall Harvest Fruit Salad	95
Mixed Fruit Salad	96
Creamy Fruit-Pecan Salad	97
Scalloped Carrots and Celery	98
Easy Creamed Green Beans	99
Hawaiian Apple Salad	100
Creamy Peas and Corn	101

Sensational
Sides (continued)

Broccoli-Corn Dish   102

Frosted Cauliflower/Broccoli Bake   103

Broccoli and Rice Side Dish   104

Swiss Tomato-Corn Bake   105

Farmstead Corn Pudding   106

Party-Time Baked Beans   107

Mexican Potato Salad   108

Garden Cucumber Potato Salad   109

Molded Garden Salad

This may seem a bit unusual to those people used to sweet salads made with gelatin, but molded salads with vegetables, also known as aspics, are a party perennial that both look and taste delicious. Give this one a try for a spring bridal shower or late-afternoon tea, and you'll be delighted by the response. ☺ Serves 8

1 (4-serving) package JELL-O sugar-free lime gelatin

1 cup hot water

1 cup cold water

2 tablespoons cider vinegar

1 teaspoon prepared horseradish

⅛ teaspoon black pepper

1¼ cups chopped cabbage

¾ cup unpeeled chopped cucumbers

¾ cup shredded carrots

2 tablespoons chopped green bell pepper

2 tablespoons chopped radishes

Lettuce

In a medium bowl, dissolve gelatin in hot water. Stir in cold water. Mix well to dissolve gelatin. Add vinegar, horseradish, and black pepper. Mix well to combine. Stir in cabbage, cucumbers, carrots, green pepper, and radishes. Pour mixture into an 8-by-8-inch dish. Refrigerate 4 hours or until firm. Cut into 8 servings. When serving, place salad on lettuce-lined salad plates.

HINT: Good topped with 1 teaspoon fat-free mayonnaise, but don't forget to count the extra calories.

Each serving equals:

HE: ¾ Vegetable • 5 Optional Calories

16 Calories • 0 gm Fat • 1 gm Protein •
3 gm Carbohydrate • 34 mg Sodium • 1 gm Fiber

DIABETIC: 1 Free Vegetable

Gazpacho Salad

Nothing's as cool, crisp, and refreshing as gazpacho on a summer evening, but if you're looking to add a side dish instead of a cold soup to your party menu, this one is tangy like the soup that inspired it, but with the added pleasure of pasta!

○ Serves 8 (1 cup)

> 3½ cups (two 14½-ounce cans) stewed tomatoes, undrained
>
> 2 teaspoons Italian seasoning
>
> ½ teaspoon dried minced garlic
>
> 2 teaspoons vegetable oil
>
> 2 cups unpeeled diced cucumbers
>
> 1½ cups sliced celery
>
> 4 cups cold cooked rotini pasta, rinsed and drained

In a large bowl, combine undrained stewed tomatoes, Italian seasoning, garlic, and vegetable oil. Add cucumbers, celery, and pasta. Mix gently to combine. Cover and refrigerate for at least one hour. Gently stir again just before serving.

HINTS: 1. Vegetable-flavored rotini pasta works great.

2. 3 cups uncooked rotini pasta usually cooks to about 4 cups.

Each serving equals:

HE: 1¾ Vegetable • 1 Bread • ¼ Fat

150 Calories • 2 gm Fat • 5 gm Protein •
28 gm Carbohydrate • 298 mg Sodium • 1 gm Fiber

DIABETIC: 1 Vegetable • 1 Starch

Catalina Isle Salad

There's so much good "stuff" mixed up in this pretty presentation, you'll be lost in admiration at its varied flavors. Just like the famed island off the California coast that attracts visitors who return year after year, this salad will become a regular on your table.

○ Serves 8 (1 cup)

> 4 cups cold cooked elbow macaroni, rinsed and drained
> 1½ cups diced fresh tomato
> ½ cup chopped onion
> ½ cup chopped celery
> ½ cup chopped green bell pepper
> ½ cup chopped radishes
> ¾ cup (3 ounces) shredded Kraft reduced-fat Cheddar cheese
> 2 tablespoons Hormel Bacon Bits
> ¾ cup Kraft Fat Free Catalina Dressing
> ¼ cup Kraft fat-free mayonnaise
> ⅛ teaspoon black pepper

In a large bowl, combine macaroni, tomato, onion, celery, green pepper, radishes, Cheddar cheese, and bacon bits. Add Catalina dressing, mayonnaise, and black pepper. Mix well to combine. Cover and refrigerate for at least 30 minutes. Gently stir again just before serving.

HINT: 1⅓ cups uncooked macaroni usually cooks to 2 cups.

Each serving equals:

HE: 1 Bread • ¾ Vegetable • ½ Protein • ½ Slider • 3 Optional Calories

178 Calories • 2 gm Fat • 7 gm Protein • 33 gm Carbohydrate • 401 mg Sodium • 2 gm Fiber

DIABETIC: 1½ Starch • ½ Vegetable • ½ Meat • *or* 2 Carbohydrate • ½ Meat

Grande Bean and Carrot Toss

It'll take you less than a minute to stir up this spicy summer salad, but the great flavors will linger in pleasurable memories! If you consider yourself an inexperienced party giver, put this one on the menu. It's so quick and easy, even kids can make it, but the look and taste is all grown-up. ☻ Serves 8 (1 cup)

  1 cup chunky salsa (mild, medium, or hot)
  1 cup Kraft Fat Free Catalina Dressing
  4 cups (two 16-ounce cans) sliced carrots, rinsed and drained
  4 cups (two 16-ounce cans) cut green beans, rinsed and drained
  ¾ cup (3 ounces) shredded Kraft reduced-fat Cheddar cheese

In a large bowl, combine salsa and Catalina dressing. Add carrots, green beans, and Cheddar cheese. Mix gently to coat. Cover and refrigerate for at least 2 hours. Gently stir again just before serving.

Each serving equals:

HE: 2¼ Vegetable • ½ Protein • ½ Slider •
10 Optional Calories

---

106 Calories • 2 gm Fat • 4 gm Protein •
18 gm Carbohydrate • 524 mg Sodium • 2 gm Fiber

DIABETIC: 3 Vegetable • ½ Meat *or*
1 Carbohydrate • ½ Meat

Mustard Cucumber Salad

What's so special about Dijon mustard that this recipe calls for it instead of the good old American yellow stuff? A quick taste will tell you it's got a wonderfully rich flavor and will add so much to any salad dressing. If your garden overflows with cucumbers this year, offer this dish at your next barbecue!

○ Serves 8 (½ cup)

> 2 tablespoons Dijon mustard
>
> ¾ cup Kraft fat-free mayonnaise
>
> ¼ cup skim milk
>
> 2 teaspoons dried parsley flakes
>
> Sugar substitute to equal 1 tablespoon sugar
>
> ⅛ teaspoon black pepper
>
> 3½ cups unpeeled thinly sliced cucumbers
>
> ½ cup sliced onion

In a large bowl, combine mustard, mayonnaise, skim milk, parsley flakes, sugar substitute, and black pepper. Add cucumbers and onions. Mix gently to combine. Cover and refrigerate for at least 1 hour. Gently stir again just before serving.

Each serving equals:

HE: 1 Vegetable • 18 Optional Calories

29 Calories • 1 gm Fat • 0 gm Protein • 5 gm Carbohydrate • 258 mg Sodium • 0 gm Fiber

DIABETIC: 1 Vegetable

Rainbow Tossed Salad

The name says it all—lots of simple ingredients, tossed into a pretty bowl, then blended with a creamy dressing that tastes like a special treat. Your guests will love "eating their vegetables" when you serve them up like this! ☙ Serves 8 (1½ cups)

8 cups shredded iceberg lettuce
2 cups frozen peas, thawed
¾ cup (3 ounces) shredded Kraft reduced-fat Cheddar cheese
2 cups grated carrots
3 tablespoons Hormel Bacon Bits
½ cup sliced radishes
½ cup chopped green onion
⅓ cup Kraft Fat Free Thousand Island Dressing
¼ cup Kraft fat-free mayonnaise
½ teaspoon lemon pepper

In a large bowl, combine lettuce, peas, Cheddar cheese, carrots, bacon bits, radishes, and green onion. In a small bowl, combine Thousand Island dressing, mayonnaise, and lemon pepper. Add dressing mixture to lettuce mixture. Mix gently to combine. Serve at once.

HINT: Thaw peas by placing in a colander and rinsing under hot water for one minute.

Each serving equals:
HE: 2¾ Vegetable • ½ Bread • ½ Protein • ¼ Slider • 2 Optional Calories

110 Calories • 2 gm Fat • 7 gm Protein •
16 gm Carbohydrate • 290 mg Sodium • 3 gm Fiber

DIABETIC: 1½ Starch • ½ Vegetable • ½ Meat • ½ Fat

Dill Pickle-Cheese Salad Toss

I love salads that deliver a surprise, especially when you're expecting a basic bowl of greens and you find pickles, chopped nuts, and mozzarella cheese mixed into the garden! This dressing is a real winner with pickle lovers—are there any at your house?

◯ Serves 8 (1 full cup)

8 cups bite-size pieces of assorted salad greens

8 dill pickle spears, cut into bite-size pieces

¾ cup (3 ounces) shredded Kraft reduced-fat mozzarella cheese

½ cup (2 ounces) chopped dry-roasted peanuts

2 teaspoons vegetable oil

⅓ cup dill pickle juice

⅛ teaspoon black pepper

In a large bowl, combine salad greens, dill pickle pieces, mozzarella cheese, and peanuts. In a covered jar, combine vegetable oil, pickle juice, and black pepper. Shake well to blend. Pour dressing mixture evenly over greens. Toss gently to coat. Serve at once.

Each serving equals:

HE: 2 Vegetable • ¾ Fat • ¾ Protein

90 Calories • 6 gm Fat • 5 gm Protein •
4 gm Carbohydrate • 130 mg Sodium • 2 gm Fiber

DIABETIC: 1 Vegetable • 1 Fat • ½ Meat

French Copper Pennies

The name of this dish comes from an old-timey carrot recipe that compares those orange rounds to colorful coins. My version mingles their crunchy sweetness with a tangy-sweet dressing that makes them extra-special, and pretty for a buffet.

● Serves 8 (full ¾ cup)

> 6 cups (three 16-ounce cans) sliced carrots, rinsed and drained
> ½ cup finely diced red onion
> ½ cup finely chopped green bell pepper
> ¾ cup Kraft Fat Free French Dressing
> 1 tablespoon dried parsley flakes
> 1 tablespoon Brown Sugar Twin
> ½ teaspoon prepared mustard

In a large bowl, combine carrots, onion, and green pepper. In a small bowl, combine French dressing, parsley flakes, Brown Sugar Twin, and mustard. Mix well to combine. Refrigerate for at least 30 minutes. Gently stir again just before serving.

Each serving equals:

HE: 1¾ Vegetable • ¼ Slider • 8 Optional Calories

68 Calories • 0 gm Fat • 1 gm Protein •
16 gm Carbohydrate • 214 mg Sodium • 2 gm Fiber

DIABETIC: 2 Vegetable

Blue Cheese Mushroom Salad

There's something magical about the combination of fresh mushrooms and blue cheese dressing. I can't explain it but I know it's true, and so I created this dish to celebrate that delectable union, tossed with a few colorful shreds of carrot and green onion to tickle your tastebuds. ● Serves 8 (¾ cup)

4 cups sliced fresh mushrooms

1½ cups shredded carrots

½ cup sliced green onion

½ cup Kraft Fat Free Blue Cheese Dressing

¼ cup Kraft fat-free mayonnaise

1 teaspoon dried parsley flakes

In a large bowl, combine mushrooms, carrots, and green onion. In a small bowl, combine blue cheese dressing, mayonnaise, and parsley flakes. Add dressing mixture to vegetable mixture. Mix gently to combine. Refrigerate for at least 30 minutes. Gently stir again just before serving.

Each serving equals:

HE: 1½ Vegetable • ¼ Slider • 10 Optional Calories

40 Calories • 0 gm Fat • 1 gm Protein •
9 gm Carbohydrate • 181 mg Sodium • 1 gm Fiber

DIABETIC: 2 Vegetable

Colorful Cauliflower Buffet Salad

So much crunch for so few calories—it seems impossible, but it's true, and truly delicious. I bet your guests will pile this high onto their plates when they spot those raisins and bits of bacon!

○ Serves 8 (½ cup)

> 2¼ cups fresh cut cauliflower
> 2¼ cups fresh cut broccoli
> ½ cup chopped onion
> ½ cup raisins
> 2 tablespoons Hormel Bacon Bits
> ½ cup Kraft fat-free mayonnaise
> 2 tablespoons vinegar
> Sugar substitute to equal 2 tablespoons sugar

In a large bowl, combine cauliflower, broccoli, onion, raisins, and bacon bits. In a small bowl, combine mayonnaise, vinegar, and sugar substitute. Add mayonnaise mixture to vegetable mixture. Mix well to combine. Cover and refrigerate for at least 1 hour. Gently stir again just before serving.

Each serving equals:

HE: 1¼ Vegetable • ½ Fruit • 18 Optional Calories

64 Calories • 0 gm Fat • 2 gm Protein •
14 gm Carbohydrate • 156 mg Sodium • 2 gm Fiber

DIABETIC: 1½ Vegetable • ½ Fruit *or*
1 Carbohydrate

Carrot-Pineapple Toss

Carrots and pineapple make a marvelous marriage, all that color and sweetness combined to create a memorable dish. Add a few raisins for texture and some creamy mayonnaise, and you've got a party on a plate! ◑ Serves 8 (full ½ cup)

> 2 cups (two 8-ounce cans) pineapple tidbits, packed in fruit juice,
>   drained, and 2 tablespoons liquid reserved
> ½ cup raisins
> 4 cups shredded carrots
> ⅔ cup Kraft fat-free mayonnaise

In a medium bowl, combine pineapple, raisins, and carrots. Add mayonnaise and reserved pineapple liquid. Mix well to combine. Cover and refrigerate for at least 30 minutes. Gently stir again just before serving.

HINTS: 1. If you can't find tidbits, use chunk pineapple and coarsely chop.

2. To plump up raisins without "cooking," place in a glass measuring cup and microwave on HIGH for 20 seconds.

Each serving equals:

HE: 1 Vegetable • 1 Fruit • 13 Optional Calories

104 Calories • 0 gm Fat • 1 gm Protein •
25 gm Carbohydrate • 160 mg Sodium • 2 gm Fiber

DIABETIC: 2 Vegetable • 1 Fruit

Cherry Waldorf Salad

The classic Waldorf salad, which may have originated at the great New York hotel, inspired this beautiful gelatin salad that's just full of crunch! With its pretty red color, it would be a winner on a holiday buffet table, served alongside a fresh green salad.

○ Serves 8

> 1 (4-serving) package JELL-O sugar-free cherry gelatin
> 1 cup boiling water
> ¾ cup cold water
> 1 cup (2 small) cored, unpeeled, and diced Red Delicious apples
> 1 cup (1 medium) diced banana
> 1 cup chopped celery
> ¼ cup (1 ounce) chopped pecans

In a large bowl, combine dry gelatin and boiling water. Mix well to dissolve gelatin. Stir in cold water. Add apples, banana, celery, and pecans. Mix gently to combine. Pour mixture into an 8-by-8-inch dish. Refrigerate until firm, about 3 hours. Cut into 8 servings.

HINTS: 1. To prevent banana from turning brown, mix with 1 teaspoon lemon juice or sprinkle with Fruit Fresh.

2. Good topped with 1 tablespoon Cool Whip Lite, but don't forget to count the few additional calories.

Each serving equals:

HE: ½ Fruit • ½ Fat • ¼ Vegetable • 5 Optional Calories

54 Calories • 2 gm Fiber • 1 gm Protein •
8 gm Carbohydrate • 40 mg Sodium • 1 gm Fiber

DIABETIC: ½ Fruit • ½ Fat

Apricot Salad

There's something wonderfully special about apricots, those small golden fruits with the taste of sweet nectar. Blending them into a creamy concoction flavored with lemon and pineapple just ups the ante, giving you a luscious dish that both looks and tastes festive!

○ Serves 8

> 1 cup Diet 7UP
>
> 1 (4-serving) package JELL-O sugar-free lemon gelatin
>
> ½ cup (4 ounces) Philadelphia fat-free cream cheese
>
> 1 cup (one 8-ounce can) crushed pineapple, packed in fruit juice, undrained
>
> ¾ cup Yoplait plain fat-free yogurt
>
> ⅓ cup Carnation Nonfat Dry Milk Powder
>
> 2 cups (one 16-ounce can) apricot halves, packed in fruit juice, drained, coarsely chopped, and 2 tablespoons liquid reserved
>
> ⅓ cup Kraft fat-free mayonnaise

In a medium saucepan, bring Diet 7UP to a boil. Remove from heat. Add dry gelatin. Mix well to dissolve gelatin. Place saucepan on a wire rack and allow to cool for 15 minutes. In a large bowl, stir cream cheese with a spoon until soft. Add undrained pineapple, yogurt, and dry milk powder. Mix well using a wire whisk. Blend in chopped apricots. Add cooled gelatin mixture. Mix well to combine. Pour mixture into an 8-by-8-inch dish. Refrigerate for 3 hours or until firm. In a small bowl, combine mayonnaise and reserved apricot liquid. Evenly spread mayonnaise mixture over top. Cut into 8 servings.

Each serving equals:

HE: ¾ Fruit • ¼ Skim Milk • ¼ Protein •
11 Optional Calories

---

144 Calories • 0 gm Fat • 6 gm Protein •
30 gm Carbohydrate • 217 mg Sodium • 3 gm Fiber

DIABETIC: 1 Fruit • ½ Meat

Peachy Keen Salad

I don't know who first coined the old-fashioned slang phrase, "peachy keen," but it seemed perfect to describe this scrumptious salad! You'll be pleased at how the Cool Whip blends beautifully with the yogurt to produce a dish that's oh-so-smooth and pleasing to the eye! ❍ Serves 8 (½ cup)

> 1 (4-serving) package JELL-O sugar-free lemon gelatin
> 1 cup (one 8-ounce can) crushed pineapple, packed in fruit juice, undrained
> 1 (8-ounce) package Philadelphia fat-free cream cheese
> 2 cups (one 16-ounce can) sliced peaches, packed in fruit juice, drained and chopped
> ¾ cup Yoplait plain fat-free yogurt
> ⅓ cup Carnation Nonfat Dry Milk Powder
> 1 cup Cool Whip Lite

In a medium saucepan, combine dry gelatin and undrained pineapple. Bring mixture to a boil. Place pan on a wire rack and allow to cool for 15 minutes. In a large bowl, stir cream cheese with a spoon until soft. Add cooled gelatin mixture and peaches. Mix well to combine. In a small bowl, combine yogurt and dry milk powder. Fold in Cool Whip Lite. Stir yogurt mixture into cream cheese mixture. Refrigerate for at least 30 minutes.

Each serving equals:

HE: ¾ Fruit • ½ Protein • ¼ Skim Milk • ¼ Slider • 5 Optional Calories

105 Calories • 1 gm Fat • 7 gm Protein •
17 gm Carbohydrate • 220 mg Sodium • 0 gm Fiber

DIABETIC: 1 Fruit • ½ Meat

Fall Harvest Fruit Salad

Are you one of those people who gets a special glow every fall when the leaves begin to change and the fresh fruits of the season ripen into incredible sweetness? I invented this salad for those of you who can't get enough of autumn—the season or the flavors—and I hope you'll agree I captured its clear, sweet charm!

○ Serves 8 (½ cup)

> 1½ cups (3 small) cored, unpeeled, and diced pears
> 1½ cups (3 small) cored, unpeeled, and diced Red Delicious
>   apples
> 1 cup (6 ounces) seedless green grapes, halved
> ⅓ cup Kraft fat-free mayonnaise
> ⅓ cup Cool Whip Lite
> 1 teaspoon lemon juice
> Sugar substitute to equal 1 tablespoon sugar
> ¼ teaspoon ground cinnamon

In a large bowl, combine pears, apples, and grapes. In a small bowl, combine mayonnaise, Cool Whip Lite, lemon juice, sugar substitute, and cinnamon. Add mayonnaise mixture to fruit mixture. Mix well to combine. Refrigerate for at least 30 minutes. Gently stir again just before serving.

Each serving equals:

HE: 1 Fruit • 14 Optional Calories

64 Calories • 0 gm Fat • 0 gm Protein •
16 gm Carbohydrate • 73 mg Sodium • 1 gm Fiber

DIABETIC: 1 Fruit

Mixed Fruit Salad

So many scrumptious flavors, blended together to create a dish that's simply better than any of them could taste alone! The vanilla extract combines with the yogurt and milk powder to give this salad an extra-special goodness.   ● Serves 8 (¾ cup)

> 1 (4-serving) package JELL-O sugar-free instant vanilla pudding
>   mix
> 1¼ cups water
> 1 cup (one 8-ounce can) pineapple chunks, packed in fruit juice,
>   drained, and ¼ cup liquid reserved
> 1 cup (1 medium) diced banana
> 1 cup (2 small) cored, unpeeled, and diced Red Delicious apples
> 1 cup (one 11-ounce can) mandarin oranges, rinsed and drained
> ¼ cup (1 ounce) chopped pecans

In a large bowl, combine dry pudding mix, water, and reserved pineapple liquid. Mix well using a wire whisk. Stir in pineapple, banana, apples, and mandarin oranges. Add pecans. Mix gently to combine. Refrigerate for at least 30 minutes. Gently stir again just before serving.

HINT: To prevent banana from turning brown, mix with 1 teaspoon lemon juice or sprinkle with Fruit Fresh.

Each serving equals:

HE: 1 Fruit • ¼ Fat • 12 Optional Calories

94 Calories • 2 gm Fat • 1 gm Protein •
18 gm Carbohydrate • 167 mg Sodium • 1 gm Fiber

DIABETIC: 1 Fruit • ½ Fat

Creamy Fruit-Pecan Salad

It's creamy and crunchy, it's tangy and sweet, it's fast and it's flavorful—as the song goes, "Who could ask for anything more?" Have you noticed I like to include pecans in many of my Healthy Exchanges recipes? It's true—I'm "nuts" about them, and I bet you will be too!   ○   Serves 8 (¾ cup)

2 cups (4 small) cored, unpeeled, and diced Red Delicious apples
2 cups (2 medium) sliced bananas
1 tablespoon lemon juice
2 cups (two 8-ounce cans) pineapple tidbits, packed in fruit juice, drained
½ cup raisins
¼ cup (1 ounce) chopped pecans
¾ cup Yoplait plain fat-free yogurt
⅓ cup Carnation Nonfat Dry Milk Powder
½ cup Cool Whip Lite
1 teaspoon vanilla extract
Sugar substitute to equal 2 tablespoons sugar

In a medium bowl, combine apples and bananas. Pour lemon juice over fruit and mix gently to coat. Stir in pineapple, raisins, and pecans. In a small bowl, combine yogurt and dry milk powder. Add Cool Whip Lite, vanilla extract, and sugar substitute. Mix well to combine. Fold yogurt mixture into fruit mixture. Refrigerate for at least 30 minutes. Gently stir again just before serving.

HINT: If you can't find tidbits, use chunk pineapple and coarsely chop.

Each serving equals:

HE: 2 Fruit • ½ Fat • ¼ Skim Milk •
11 Optional Calories

179 Calories • 3 gm Fat • 3 gm Protein •
35 gm Carbohydrate • 35 mg Sodium • 2 gm Fiber

DIABETIC: 2 Fruit • ½ Fat

Scalloped Carrots and Celery

Here's an original way to add more healthy vegetables to your menu, but prepared in a truly scrumptious way. Cliff loves scalloped potatoes, so I will sometimes create a scalloped veggie dish for his approval. This one was a hit with my truck drivin' man!

⊙ Serves 8

3½ cups thinly sliced carrots

2 cups diced celery

2 cups hot water

⅔ cup Carnation Nonfat Dry Milk Powder

1⅔ cups water

3 tablespoons all-purpose flour

¾ cup (3 ounces) shredded Kraft reduced-fat Cheddar cheese

½ cup (one 2.5-ounce jar) sliced mushrooms, drained

¼ teaspoon lemon pepper

½ cup + 1 tablespoon (2¼ ounces) dried fine bread crumbs

Preheat oven to 375 degrees. Spray a 9-by-13-inch baking dish with butter-flavored cooking spray. In a large saucepan, combine carrots, celery, and water. Cook for 20 minutes or until vegetables are just tender. Drain. In a covered jar, combine dry milk powder, water, and flour. Shake well to blend. Pour milk mixture into same saucepan, now sprayed with butter-flavored cooking spray. Stir in Cheddar cheese. Cook over medium heat, stirring often, until mixture starts to thicken. Add mushrooms and lemon pepper. Mix well to combine. Stir in drained vegetables. Pour mixture into prepared baking dish. Evenly sprinkle bread crumbs over top. Bake for 45 minutes. Place pan on a wire rack and let set for 5 minutes. Divide into 8 servings.

Each serving equals:

HE: 1½ Vegetable • ½ Protein • ½ Bread • ¼ Skim Milk

106 Calories • 2 gm Fat • 7 gm Protein •
15 gm Carbohydrate • 262 mg Sodium • 2 gm Fiber

DIABETIC: 1 Vegetable • ½ Meat • ½ Starch • ½ Skim Milk
or 1 Vegetable • 1 Starch • ½ Meat

Easy Creamed Green Beans

Everyone seems to love this easy, creamy vegetable dish, and no
matter how often it appears on the menu, there are *never* any leftovers! I guess that's because it tastes rich and features the favorite
vegetable of most men I know.   ⊙ Serves 8 (⅔ cup)

1 (8-ounce) package Philadelphia fat-free cream cheese
¼ cup skim milk
¼ teaspoon lemon pepper
6 cups (three 16-ounce cans) French-style green beans, rinsed
and drained

In a large saucepan, combine cream cheese, skim milk, and
lemon pepper. Cook over medium heat, stirring often, until mixture
is smooth. Add green beans. Mix well to combine. Lower heat and
simmer 5 minutes.

Each serving equals:

HE: 1½ Vegetable • ½ Protein • 3 Optional Calories

44 Calories • 0 gm Fat • 5 gm Protein •
6 gm Carbohydrate • 176 mg Sodium • 1 gm Fiber

DIABETIC: 1 Vegetable • ½ Meat

Hawaiian Apple Salad

This is a wonderful summer salad, creamy and golden, crunchy and smooth—and just right for a family reunion on a sunny day. If you've never been to Maui, and you won't be heading out there anytime soon (just like most of us!), you can revel in the sweet island flavors in this dish.   ● Serves 8 (½ cup)

> 1 (4-serving) package JELL-O sugar-free vanilla cook-and-serve pudding mix
> 1 (4-serving) package JELL-O sugar-free lemon gelatin
> 1 cup water
> 1 cup (one 8-ounce can) crushed pineapple, packed in fruit juice, undrained
> 3 cups (6 small) cored, unpeeled, and chopped Red Delicious apples
> ¼ cup (1 ounce) chopped pecans
> 1 cup Cool Whip Lite
> 1 teaspoon coconut extract

In a medium saucepan, combine dry pudding mix, dry gelatin, water, and undrained pineapple. Bring mixture to a boil, stirring constantly. Remove from heat and refrigerate for 30 minutes. In a large bowl, combine apples and pecans. Stir in cooled pudding mixture. Gently blend in Cool Whip Lite and coconut extract. Refrigerate for at least 1 hour. Gently stir again just before serving.

Each serving equals:

HE: 1 Fruit • ½ Fat • ¼ Slider • 15 Optional Calories

99 Calories • 3 gm Fat • 1 gm Protein •
17 gm Carbohydrate • 192 mg Sodium • 1 gm Fiber

DIABETIC: 1 Fruit • 1 Fat

Creamy Peas and Corn

Fresh vegetables are delicious and healthy, but don't forget about the great taste and nutrition in frozen veggies, too. They're frozen at their ripest and sweetest, all ready for you to thaw and enjoy. When you combine them with sour cream and spices, you've got a buffet favorite every time! ❂ Serves 8 (½ cup)

   2 cups frozen whole kernel corn, thawed
   2 cups frozen peas, thawed
   1 tablespoon dried onion flakes
   1 teaspoon dried parsley flakes
   ½ cup Land O Lakes no-fat sour cream
   2 teaspoons Sugar Twin or Sprinkle Sweet
   ⅛ teaspoon black pepper

In a medium saucepan, combine corn and peas. Add onion flakes and parsley flakes. Mix well to combine. Stir in sour cream, Sugar Twin, and black pepper. Stir gently to coat. Cook for 5 minutes or until mixture is heated through, stirring occasionally.

HINT: Thaw corn and peas by placing in a colander and rinsing under hot water for one minute.

Each serving equals:

HE: 1 Bread • ¼ Slider

84 Calories • 0 gm Fat • 4 gm Protein •
17 gm Carbohydrate • 24 mg Sodium • 3 gm Fiber

DIABETIC: 1 Starch

Broccoli-Corn Dish

There's something about a baked broccoli casserole that makes even those who turn their noses up at broccoli dig in and lick their plates! Maybe it's the creamed corn that makes it so delicious, or the corn-flake crunch that wins this dish so many votes! It's one of my favorite candidates when I'm cooking for a crowd!

● Serves 8

> 2 (16-ounce) packages frozen cut broccoli, thawed
> 4 cups (two 16-ounce cans) cream-style corn
> ⅔ cup Carnation Nonfat Dry Milk Powder
> ¾ cup water
> 2 eggs, slightly beaten, or equivalent in egg substitute
> ½ teaspoon lemon pepper
> 1 cup (1½ ounces) crushed cornflakes

Preheat oven to 350 degrees. Spray a 9-by-13-inch baking dish with butter-flavored cooking spray. In a large bowl, combine broccoli and corn. In a small bowl, combine dry milk powder, water, and eggs. Add milk mixture to broccoli mixture. Mix well to combine. Stir in lemon pepper. Pour mixture into prepared baking dish. Evenly sprinkle crushed cornflakes over top. Lightly spray top with butter-flavored cooking spray. Bake for 40 to 45 minutes. Place baking dish on a wire rack and let set for 5 minutes. Divide into 8 servings.

HINT: Thaw broccoli by placing in a colander and rinsing under hot water for one minute.

Each serving equals:

HE: 1½ Vegetable • 1¼ Bread • ¼ Protein (limited) • ¼ Skim Milk

---

194 Calories • 2 gm Fat • 9 gm Protein • 35 gm Carbohydrate • 474 mg Sodium • 5 gm Fiber

---

DIABETIC: 1½ Vegetable • 1½ Starch

Frosted
Cauliflower/Broccoli Bake

Here's another easy baked veggie dish that blends those green and white florets with luscious Cheddar cheese. Because you're using frozen vegetables, your preparation time is surprisingly quick.

◐ Serves 8

2 (16-ounce) packages frozen broccoli and cauliflower blend
    pieces
3 cups hot water
1 cup Kraft fat-free mayonnaise
1 tablespoon prepared mustard
½ teaspoon lemon pepper
2 teaspoons dried parsley flakes
1½ cups (6 ounces) shredded Kraft reduced-fat Cheddar cheese

Preheat oven to 375 degrees. Spray a 9-by-13-inch baking dish with butter-flavored cooking spray. In a large saucepan, cook broccoli and cauliflower in water for 10 minutes or just until tender. Drain. In a large bowl, combine mayonnaise, mustard, lemon pepper, and parsley flakes. Add drained vegetables. Mix gently to combine. Pour mixture into prepared baking dish. Sprinkle Cheddar cheese evenly over top. Bake for 20 minutes. Divide into 8 servings.

Each serving equals:

HE: 2 Vegetable • 1 Protein • ¼ Slider

107 Calories • 3 gm Fat • 8 gm Protein •
12 gm Carbohydrate • 475 mg Sodium • 2 gm Fiber

DIABETIC: 2 Vegetable • 1 Meat

Broccoli and Rice Side Dish

Rice makes a great base for a filling accompaniment to lots of party entrees, especially when it's combined with so many good tastes in one big casserole. I like the spicy, creamy goodness of the soup joined to the tomato sauce and chili seasoning—lots of color, lots of flavor, lots of applause!   ☻   Serves 8

3½ cups frozen broccoli, thawed

3 cups cold cooked rice

1½ cups (6 ounces) shredded Kraft reduced-fat Cheddar cheese☆

1¾ cups (one 15-ounce can) Hunt's Chunky Tomato Sauce

1 (10¾-ounce) can Healthy Request Cream of Mushroom Soup

2 teaspoons dried onion flakes

2 teaspoons chili seasoning mix

Preheat oven to 350 degrees. Spray a 9-by-13-inch baking dish with butter-flavored cooking spray. In a large bowl, combine broccoli, rice, and 1 cup Cheddar cheese. Add tomato sauce, mushroom soup, onion flakes, and chili seasoning mix. Mix well to combine. Spread mixture into prepared baking dish. Bake for 30 minutes. Evenly sprinkle remaining ½ cup Cheddar cheese over top and continue baking for 10 minutes or until cheese starts to melt. Place baking dish on a wire rack and let set for 5 minutes. Divide into 8 servings.

HINTS: 1. Thaw broccoli by placing in a colander and rinsing under hot water for one minute.

2. 2 cups uncooked rice usually cooks to about 3 cups.

Each serving equals:

HE: 1¾ Vegetable • 1 Protein • ¾ Bread • ¼ Slider •
1 Optional Calorie

176 Calories • 4 gm Fat • 11 gm Protein •
24 gm Carbohydrate • 694 mg Sodium • 3 gm Fiber

DIABETIC: 1½ Vegetable • 1 Meat • 1 Starch

Swiss Tomato-Corn Bake

If you usually save stuffing for holiday meals, I hope you'll give this casserole a try at your next family gathering. It mingles so many rich flavors, especially the Swiss cheese and ham, that it would also make a good entree for a cozy winter supper.

● Serves 8

> 3½ cups (two 14½-ounce cans) stewed tomatoes, undrained
> ½ cup chopped onion
> 2 cups frozen whole kernel corn, thawed
> ¼ teaspoon black pepper
> 2 cups (3 ounces) Pepperidge Farm dried bread cubes
> 1 full cup (6 ounces) diced Dubuque 97% fat-free ham or any
>   extra-lean ham
> 4 (¾-ounce) slices Kraft or Weight Watchers reduced-fat Swiss
>   cheese, shredded

Preheat oven to 350 degrees. Spray a 9-by-13-inch baking dish with butter-flavored cooking spray. In a large bowl, combine undrained stewed tomatoes, onion, corn, and black pepper. Stir in bread cubes. Add ham and Swiss cheese. Mix well to combine. Pour mixture into prepared baking dish. Bake for 30 minutes. Place baking dish on a wire rack and let set for 5 minutes. Cut into 8 servings.

HINT: Thaw corn by placing in a colander and rinsing under hot water for one minute.

Each serving equals:

HE: 1 Bread • 1 Protein • 1 Vegetable

---

168 Calories • 4 gm Fat • 8 gm Protein •
25 gm Carbohydrate • 670 mg Sodium • 4 gm Fiber

DIABETIC: 1 Starch • 1 Meat • 1 Vegetable

Farmstead Corn Pudding

Here's a dish that no one can believe is truly healthy, because it's just so creamy and rich, it tastes as if it's got butter and cream mixed in! The two kinds of corn make it especially "corn-y" for all you fans of the "kernel." This looks great on a buffet table, and its aroma will bring guests running before you ring the dinner bell!

○ Serves 8

> 2 cups (one 16-ounce can) cream-style corn
> 2 cups (one 16-ounce can) whole kernel corn, rinsed and drained
> ¾ cup chopped red onion
> ¼ cup chopped green bell pepper
> ⅔ cup Carnation Nonfat Dry Milk Powder
> ½ cup water
> 6 tablespoons (1½ ounces) dried fine bread crumbs
> ¾ cup (3 ounces) shredded Kraft reduced-fat Cheddar cheese
> 2 tablespoons Hormel Bacon Bits

Preheat oven to 350 degrees. Spray a 9-by-13-inch baking dish with butter-flavored cooking spray. In a large bowl, combine cream-style corn, whole kernel corn, onion, and green pepper. Add dry milk powder and water. Mix well to combine. Stir in bread crumbs, Cheddar cheese, and bacon bits. Spread mixture evenly into prepared baking dish. Bake for 40 to 45 minutes. Place baking dish on a wire rack and let set for 5 minutes. Divide into 8 servings.

Each serving equals:

> HE: 1¼ Bread • ½ Protein • ¼ Skim Milk • ¼ Vegetable
> • 6 Optional Calories
>
> 162 Calories • 2 gm Fat • 8 gm Protein •
> 28 gm Carbohydrate • 494 mg Sodium • 1 gm Fiber
>
> DIABETIC: 1½ Starch • ½ Meat

Party-Time Baked Beans

Baked beans are a great party food, and my healthy version cuts out the extra fat and sugar but stirs in lots of smoky rich flavor and that New England tanginess only maple syrup flavor can provide. If you've only tried the canned kind of baked beans, this dish will delight you for years to come. ● Serves 8

30 ounces (three 16-ounce cans) great northern beans, rinsed and drained

1 (10¾-ounce) can Healthy Request Tomato Soup

1 cup (one 8-ounce can) Hunt's Tomato Sauce

¼ cup Cary's Sugar Free Maple Syrup

¼ cup hot dog relish

2 teaspoons dried onion flakes

1½ cups (9 ounces) finely diced Dubuque 97% fat-free ham or any extra-lean ham

Preheat oven to 350 degrees. Spray a 9-by-13-inch baking dish with butter-flavored cooking spray. In a large bowl, combine great northern beans, tomato soup, tomato sauce, and maple syrup. Add hot dog relish, onion flakes, and ham. Mix well to combine. Spread mixture into prepared baking dish. Bake for 45 to 50 minutes. Place baking dish on a wire rack and let set for 5 minutes. Divide into 8 servings.

HINT: If you don't have hot dog relish, use 2 tablespoons dill pickle relish and 1 teaspoon prepared mustard.

Each serving equals:

HE: 2⅔ Protein • ½ Vegetable • ¼ Slider • 15 Optional Calories

202 Calories • 2 gm Fat • 13 gm Protein • 33 gm Carbohydrate • 577 mg Sodium • 8 gm Fiber

DIABETIC: 2 Starch • 1½ Meat

Mexican Potato Salad

Dazzle your friends with a surprising new kind of potato salad—a cheesy, spicy, South-of-the-Border stunner that couldn't be tastier! The Ranch dressing is a cool addition that goes great alongside the salsa! ● Serves 8 (¾ cup)

> 5 cups (24 ounces) diced cooked potatoes
> ¾ cup (3 ounces) shredded Kraft reduced-fat Cheddar cheese
> 1 cup chunky salsa (mild, medium, or hot)
> ½ cup Kraft Fat Free Ranch Dressing
> 2 tablespoons Kraft fat-free mayonnaise
> 2 teaspoons dried parsley flakes

In a large bowl, combine potatoes and Cheddar cheese. In a medium bowl, combine salsa, Ranch dressing, mayonnaise, and parsley flakes. Add salsa mixture to potato mixture. Mix gently to combine. Refrigerate for at least 30 minutes. Gently stir again just before serving.

Each serving equals:

HE: ¾ Bread • ½ Protein • ¼ Vegetable • ¼ Slider • 7 Optional Calories

125 Calories • 1 gm Fat • 5 gm Protein • 24 gm Carbohydrate • 377 mg Sodium • 1 gm Fiber

DIABETIC: 1½ Starch *or* Carbohydrate • ½ Meat

Garden Cucumber Potato Salad

Here's another great change from traditional potato salad, perfect for a big family picnic or any summer celebration. The red onions and radishes lend lovely color to the dish, and lemon pepper finishes it off perfectly. ◔ Serves 8 (¾ cup)

4½ cups (24 ounces) thinly sliced cooked potatoes
1 cup thinly sliced radishes
½ cup thinly sliced red onion
1½ cups unpeeled thinly sliced cucumbers
⅔ cup Kraft fat-free mayonnaise
½ teaspoon lemon pepper
Sugar substitute to equal 2 tablespoons sugar
1 teaspoon dried parsley flakes

In a large bowl, combine potatoes, radishes, onion, and cucumbers. In a small bowl, combine mayonnaise, lemon pepper, sugar substitute, and parsley flakes. Add mayonnaise mixture to potato mixture. Mix gently to combine. Cover and refrigerate for at least 30 minutes. Gently stir again just before serving.

Each serving equals:

HE: ¾ Bread • ¾ Vegetable • 15 Optional Calories

96 Calories • 0 gm Fat • 2 gm Protein •
22 gm Carbohydrate • 147 mg Sodium • 2 gm Fiber

DIABETIC: 1 Starch • 1 Vegetable

The Main Event

When anyone asks what you're serving at your party, they're hoping to hear about the centerpiece on your buffet, whether it's a spicy Mexican casserole bubbling over with cheese or a sizzling tray of lasagna that fills the dining room with the unmistakable fragrance of an Italian ristorante. No matter what other dishes you're planning to offer, your most important decision is what you'll shine the spotlight on!

Whether you're having the Cousins Club for brunch or your co-workers for a holiday get-together, you need something fabulous, filling, and fun to eat—a taste they'll remember long after the candles have melted down and the party is just a memory. I've included a wealth of scrumptious suggestions, from healthy versions of traditional family favorites to tasty classics inspired by ethnic traditions from all over the world.

You'll find great ideas for chicken, pork, turkey, fish, and beef, plus vegetarian entrees so satisfying your guests will never miss the meat. Stirred up in only a few minutes, sautéed swiftly in a skillet or baked in the oven while you set the table, these culinary pleasures will inspire a fan club for you!

The Main Event

Ham and Eggs Pizza	113
Buffet Egg Casserole	114
Acapulco Tuna Salad	116
Macaroni and Tuna Salad	117
Company Fillets	118
Baked Chicken with Cream Sauce	119
Chicken-Apple Salad Stuffed Pitas	120
Party-Time Chicken Salad	122
Chicken Breast Cacciatore with Spaghetti	124
Harvest Dressing and Turkey	126
Cordon Bleu Rice Dish	128
Applesauce Pork Balls	130
Hawaiian Baked Pork Tenders	131
Baked Pork in Cider Gravy	132
Grande Stuffed Baked Tomatoes	133
He-Man Open-Faced Hoagies	134
Sauerkraut Pizza	135
Chop Suey Pasta Hot Dish	136
Skillet Hamburger Celery Stroganoff	137
Grande Mexican Lasagna	138
Frankfurter Spanish Rice	139
Rio Taco Pie	140
Festive Ham Salad Buns	141
Buffet Baked Ham Salad	142

The Main
Event (continued)

Hawaiian Ham Sandwiches   143

Pasta with Carrots and Ham   144

Italian Ham Rotini   145

Amoré Ham and Cheese Pie   146

Baked Ham with Island Sauce   147

Ham and Eggs Pizza

Here's a true winner that begins with that best-loved breakfast classic (ham and eggs), then reinvents it with a flaky crust, a cheesy topping, and some delicious fresh vegetables. It tastes even more delectable than it looks! ◕ Serves 8

1 (8-ounce) can Pillsbury refrigerated crescent dinner rolls

4 eggs or equivalent in egg substitute

½ teaspoon Italian seasoning

1 full cup (6 ounces) diced Dubuque 97% fat-free ham or any extra-lean ham

¾ cup (3 ounces) shredded Kraft reduced-fat mozzarella cheese

½ cup (one 2.5-ounce jar) sliced mushrooms, drained

¼ cup chopped green bell pepper

¼ cup chopped onion

2 cups diced fresh tomatoes

¼ cup (¾ ounce) grated Kraft fat-free Parmesan cheese

Preheat oven to 350 degrees. Spray a rimmed 9-by-13-inch cookie sheet with butter-flavored cooking spray. Gently pat rolls into prepared pan, being sure to seal perforations. Bake for 5 minutes. In a small bowl, combine eggs and Italian seasoning. Pour egg mixture evenly over partially baked crust. Evenly layer ham, mozzarella cheese, mushrooms, green pepper, onion, and tomatoes over egg mixture. Sprinkle Parmesan cheese evenly over top. Bake for 30 to 40 minutes or until eggs are set and crust is golden brown. Place pan on a wire rack and let set for 5 minutes. Cut into 8 servings.

Each serving equals:

HE: 1⅔ Protein (½ limited) • 1 Bread • ¾ Vegetable

233 Calories • 10 gm Fat • 17 gm Protein •
19 gm Carbohydrate • 742 mg Sodium • 2 gm Fiber

DIABETIC: 2 Meat • 1 Starch • ½ Fat

Buffet Egg Casserole

If it's just not brunch without eggs, here's a perfect way to please: a healthy "quiche"-type dish that's rich with cheese and ham, and so creamy good it's hard to believe it's made with skim milk!

○ Serves 8

2 cups (3 ounces) Brownberry unseasoned bread cubes

1½ cups (9 ounces) diced Dubuque 97% fat-free ham or
    any extra-lean ham

1½ cups (6 ounces) shredded Kraft reduced-fat
    Cheddar cheese☆

8 eggs or equivalent in egg substitute

1½ cups (one 12-fluid-ounce can) Carnation Evaporated
    Skim Milk

1 teaspoon lemon pepper

1 (10¾-ounce) can Healthy Request Cream of Mushroom Soup

⅓ cup Carnation Nonfat Dry Milk Powder

¾ cup water

Spray a 9-by-13-inch baking dish with butter-flavored cooking spray. Arrange bread cubes evenly over bottom of pan. Layer ham and 1 cup of Cheddar cheese over bread cubes. In a large bowl, combine eggs, evaporated skim milk, and lemon pepper. Mix gently to blend. Evenly pour egg mixture over top. Cover and refrigerate for at least 1 hour or up to 24 hours. Just before baking, preheat oven to 275 degrees. In a small bowl, combine mushroom soup, dry milk powder, and water. Evenly spread soup mixture over egg mixture. Sprinkle remaining ½ cup Cheddar cheese evenly over top. Bake for 1½ hours. Place baking dish on a wire rack and let set for 5 minutes. Cut into 8 servings.

Each serving equals:

HE: 2¾ Protein (1 limited) • ½ Bread • ½ Skim Milk • ¼ Slider • 1 Optional Calorie

---

245 Calories • 9 gm Fat • 22 gm Protein • 19 gm Carbohydrate • 765 mg Sodium • 1 gm Fiber

---

DIABETIC: 3 Meat • 1 Starch • ½ Skim Milk

Acapulco Tuna Salad

Corn chips in a healthy entree? I'll have you know my very first Healthy Exchanges recipe was topped with crushed corn chips, and it paved the way for thousands of scrumptious, good-for-you recipes to follow. This spicy dish is the culinary equivalent of a cruise down the Mexican Riviera! ● Serves 8

2 (6-ounce) cans white tuna, packed in water, drained and flaked
1 cup chopped green bell pepper
1 cup chopped celery
½ cup chopped onion
½ cup chunky salsa (mild, medium, or hot)
⅛ teaspoon black pepper
⅔ cup Kraft fat-free mayonnaise
1⅓ cups (4 ounces) coarsely crushed corn chips
4 cups finely shredded lettuce

In a large bowl, combine tuna, green pepper, celery, onion, salsa, black pepper, and mayonnaise. Add corn chips. Mix gently to combine. Refrigerate for at least 30 minutes. For each serving, place ½ cup shredded lettuce on serving plate and top with ½ cup tuna mixture.

Each serving equals:

HE: ¾ Vegetable • ¾ Protein • ½ Bread • ½ Slider •
13 Optional Calories

153 Calories • 5 gm Fat • 12 gm Protein •
15 gm Carbohydrate • 472 mg Sodium • 1 gm Fiber

DIABETIC: 1½ Meat • 1 Starch • 1 Free Vegetable

Macaroni and Tuna Salad

It seems that every family has a tuna and macaroni salad that's been handed down from mother to daughter over the years. Here's a healthy version of our family favorite, rich with tasty ingredients like olives and cabbage that give it a special pizazz!

● Serves 8 (1 cup)

3 cups cold cooked macaroni, rinsed and drained

½ cup (2 ounces) sliced ripe olives

2 hard-boiled eggs, sliced

2 (6-ounce) cans white tuna, packed in water, drained and flaked

2 cups finely shredded cabbage

1 cup Kraft fat-free mayonnaise

1 tablespoon prepared mustard

2 tablespoons white vinegar

⅛ teaspoon black pepper

1 teaspoon dried parsley flakes

In a large bowl, combine macaroni, olives, eggs, and tuna. Stir in cabbage. In a medium bowl, combine mayonnaise, mustard, vinegar, black pepper, and parsley flakes. Add mayonnaise mixture to macaroni mixture. Mix well to combine. Refrigerate for at least 30 minutes. Gently stir again just before serving.

HINTS: 1. 2 cups uncooked macaroni usually cooks to 3 cups.

2. If you want the look and feel of eggs without the cholesterol, toss out the yolk and dice the white.

Each serving equals:

HE: 1 Protein (¼ limited) • ¾ Bread • ½ Vegetable • ¼ Fat • ¼ Slider

171 Calories • 3 gm Fat • 15 gm Protein • 21 gm Carbohydrate • 495 mg Sodium • 1 gm Fiber

DIABETIC: 2 Meat • 1½ Starch

Company Fillets

If you're looking for a quick and easy way to serve fish to your guests, this recipe is a perfect choice! The fat-free Parmesan cheese is astonishingly rich in taste and aroma, and your kitchen will soon smell like a little piece of heaven.   ⊙ Serves 8

> 2 cups sliced onion
>
> 32 ounces white fish, cut into 8 pieces
>
> ¾ cup Kraft fat-free mayonnaise
>
> ¼ cup (¾ ounce) grated Kraft fat-free Parmesan cheese
>
> 2 tablespoons lemon juice
>
> 1 teaspoon Worcestershire sauce
>
> ½ teaspoon paprika
>
> 2 tablespoons chopped fresh parsley or 2 teaspoons dried parsley
>   flakes

Preheat oven to 350 degrees. Spray a 9-by-13-inch baking dish with butter-flavored cooking spray. In a large skillet sprayed with butter-flavored cooking spray, sauté onion for 10 minutes or until tender. Meanwhile, evenly arrange fish pieces in prepared baking dish. In a small bowl, combine mayonnaise, Parmesan cheese, lemon juice, Worcestershire sauce, and paprika. Spread mayonnaise mixture evenly over fish. Spoon sautéed onion evenly over top. Bake for 25 to 30 minutes or until fish flakes easily with a fork. Just before serving, sprinkle top with parsley.

Each serving equals:

HE: 1⅔ Protein • ½ Vegetable • 15 Optional Calories

133 Calories • 1 gm Fat • 23 gm Protein •
8 gm Carbohydrate • 294 mg Sodium • 1 gm Fiber

DIABETIC: 3 Meat • ½ Vegetable

Baked Chicken with Cream Sauce

I love recipes like this one, which simply requires well-chosen ingredients, a preheated oven, and a few moments to prepare before you close the oven door! While it bakes, you can take your time to get ready for the party, and the house will take on a luscious aroma.

● Serves 8

> 2 (2.5-ounce) packages Carl Buddig lean roast beef
> 8 (3-ounce) pieces skinned and boned uncooked chicken breasts
> 1 (10¾-ounce) can Healthy Request Cream of Mushroom Soup
> ½ cup Land O Lakes no-fat sour cream
> 1 tablespoon dried parsley flakes
> ¼ teaspoon paprika

Preheat oven to 325 degrees. Spray a 9-by-13-inch baking dish with butter-flavored cooking spray. Evenly arrange roast beef slices in prepared baking dish. Place chicken pieces over top of beef. In a medium bowl, combine mushroom soup, sour cream, and parsley flakes. Spoon soup mixture evenly over chicken pieces. Bake for 50 to 55 minutes. Lightly sprinkle paprika over top. Divide into 8 servings.

Each serving equals:

HE: 3 Protein • ¼ Slider • 16 Optional Calories

138 Calories • 2 gm Fat • 24 gm Protein •
6 gm Carbohydrate • 381 mg Sodium • 0 gm Fiber

DIABETIC: 3 Meat • ½ Starch

Chicken-Apple Salad Stuffed Pitas

I took two traditional favorites—chicken salad and Waldorf salad—and had them "shake flavors and say howdy" in this crunchy, fruity, flavorful dish that can easily be doubled or tripled for a crowd. *Mmmmm-hmmmmm!* ◐ Serves 8

> 2 cups (10 ounces) diced cooked chicken breast
>
> 2 cups (4 small) cored, unpeeled, and diced Red Delicious apples
>
> ½ cup raisins
>
> 1 cup diced celery
>
> ¼ cup (1 ounce) chopped pecans
>
> ½ cup Kraft fat-free mayonnaise
>
> 2 teaspoons lemon juice
>
> 4 pita bread rounds

In a medium bowl, combine chicken, apples, raisins, celery, and pecans. Add mayonnaise and lemon juice. Mix well to combine. Cut pita rounds in half. Stuff a full ½ cup of chicken mixture into each pita half. Refrigerate at least 15 minutes.

HINTS: 1. To plump up raisins without "cooking," place in a glass measuring cup and microwave on HIGH for 20 seconds.

2. If you don't have leftovers, purchase a chunk of cooked chicken breast from your local deli.

3. To make opening pita rounds easier, place pita halves on a paper towel and microwave on HIGH for 10 seconds. Remove and gently press open.

Each serving equals:

HE: 1¼ Protein • 1 Bread • 1 Fruit • ½ Fat • ¼ Vegetable • 10 Optional Calories

216 Calories • 4 gm Fat • 14 gm Protein • 31 gm Carbohydrate • 307 mg Sodium • 2 gm Fiber

DIABETIC: 1½ Meat • 1 Starch • 1 Fruit • ½ Fat *or* 2 Carbohydrate • 1½ Meat • ½ Fat

Party-Time Chicken Salad

When you're stirring up all the delicious ingredients in this colorful chicken dish, you're sure to remark that it looks like they're having a party in your bowl! It's amazing how much delectable crunch just a few nuts will add to this recipe's special appeal.

☻ Serves 8 (1 cup)

> 2 cups (6 ounces) uncooked elbow macaroni
> 4 cups frozen cut green beans
> 3 cups hot water
> 2 full cups (12 ounces) diced cooked chicken breast
> 2 cups chopped celery
> ½ cup (2 ounces) slivered almonds
> 2 cups (two 8-ounce cans) pineapple chunks, packed in fruit
>   juice, drained, and 2 tablespoons liquid reserved
> ¾ cup Yoplait plain fat-free yogurt
> ⅓ cup Carnation Nonfat Dry Milk Powder
> ¾ cup Kraft fat-free mayonnaise
> 2 teaspoons prepared mustard
> 2 teaspoons dried parsley flakes

In a large saucepan, combine uncooked macaroni, green beans, and water. Bring mixture to a boil. Lower heat and cook for 15 minutes or until tender, stirring occasionally. Drain. In a large bowl, combine chicken, celery, almonds, and pineapple. Stir in macaroni and green bean mixture. In a small bowl, combine yogurt, dry milk powder, and mayonnaise. Add reserved pineapple liquid, mustard, and parsley flakes. Mix well to combine. Stir yogurt mixture into chicken mixture. Cover and refrigerate for at least 30 minutes. Gently stir again just before serving.

Each serving equals:

HE: 1¾ Protein • 1½ Vegetable • 1 Bread • ½ Fruit • ½ Fat • ¼ Skim Milk • 15 Optional Calories

262 Calories • 6 gm Fat • 20 gm Protein • 32 gm Carbohydrate • 268 mg Sodium • 4 gm Fiber

DIABETIC: 2 Meat • 1½ Starch • 1 Vegetable • ½ Fruit • ½ Fat

Chicken Breast Cacciatore with Spaghetti

Here's an old-time favorite that everyone loves, a dish that never loses its sparkle as it sits in the center of your buffet table! I think you'll be pleased at how just a little seasoning makes it taste like a celebration is going on in your mouth!

● Serves 8 (1 cup)

16 ounces skinned and boned uncooked chicken breast, cut into 24 pieces
1 cup chopped onion
½ cup chopped green bell pepper
2 cups (one 16-ounce can) tomatoes, coarsely chopped and undrained
1¾ cups (one 15-ounce can) Hunt's Chunky Tomato Sauce
1 (10¾-ounce) can Healthy Request Cream of Mushroom Soup
2 teaspoons Italian seasoning
½ teaspoon dried minced garlic
⅛ teaspoon black pepper
3 cups hot cooked spaghetti, rinsed and drained

In a large skillet sprayed with olive oil–flavored cooking spray, sauté chicken, onion, and green pepper for 10 minutes. Stir in undrained tomatoes, tomato sauce, mushroom soup, Italian seasoning, garlic, and black pepper. Add spaghetti. Mix well to combine. Lower heat and simmer for 15 minutes, stirring occasionally.

HINT: 2½ cups uncooked spaghetti usually cooks to about 3 cups.

Each serving equals:

HE: 1¾ Vegetable • 1½ Protein • ¾ Bread • ¼ Slider • 1 Optional Calorie

---

178 Calories • 2 gm Fat • 17 gm Protein • 23 gm Carbohydrate • 224 mg Sodium • 2 gm Fiber

---

DIABETIC: 1½ Vegetable • 1½ Meat • 1 Starch

Harvest Dressing and Turkey

Depending on where you live in the United States, you may call that best-loved Thanksgiving side dish "dressing" or "stuffing." Whatever you call it, this is a quick way to use up leftover turkey or simply enjoy the taste you yearn for all year long! I bet that between Thanksgiving and Christmas, you'll serve this more than once. ❍ Serves 8

2 cups chopped onion

2 cups grated carrots

2 cups chopped celery

16 slices reduced-calorie day-old white bread, crumbled

2 teaspoons poultry seasoning

½ teaspoon lemon pepper

2 cups (one 16-ounce can) Healthy Request Chicken Broth

1 cup water

2 cups (10 ounces) diced cooked turkey breast

Preheat oven to 350 degrees. Spray a 9-by-13-inch baking dish with butter-flavored cooking spray. In a large skillet sprayed with butter-flavored cooking spray, sauté onion, carrots, and celery for 6 to 8 minutes, or until vegetables are tender. Add bread, poultry seasoning, and lemon pepper. Mix well to combine. Stir in chicken broth, water, and turkey. Pour mixture into prepared baking dish.

Cover and bake for 30 minutes. Uncover and continue baking for 15 minutes. Place baking dish on a wire rack and let set for 5 minutes. Divide into 8 servings.

HINTS: 1. If you don't have leftovers, purchase a chunk of cooked turkey breast from your local deli.

2. A good use for day-old bread.

Each serving equals:

HE: 1½ Vegetable • 1¼ Protein • 1 Bread • 4 Optional Calories

---

173 Calories • 1 gm Fat • 19 gm Protein • 22 gm Carbohydrate • 363 mg Sodium • 2 gm Fiber

---

DIABETIC: 1 Meat • 1 Starch • 1 Vegetable

Cordon Bleu Rice Dish

Okay, maybe you haven't been to the famous French cooking school. It's no secret that neither have I. But I've picked up a few of their secrets along the way and incorporated them into some of my Healthy Exchanges recipes. Based on the renowned dish called Chicken Cordon Bleu, this recipe dazzles with its rich flavors of chicken, cheese, and ham. ● Serves 8 (1 cup)

2 full cups (12 ounces) diced cooked turkey breast

2 full cups (12 ounces) diced Dubuque 97% fat-free ham or any extra-lean ham

2 cups (one 16-ounce can) Healthy Request Chicken Broth

⅔ cup Carnation Nonfat Dry Milk Powder

1 cup water

3 tablespoons all-purpose flour

2 tablespoons Dijon mustard

4 cups (two 16-ounce cans) cut green beans, rinsed and drained

1 cup (3 ounces) uncooked instant rice

¾ cup (3 ounces) shredded Kraft reduced-fat Cheddar cheese

In a large skillet sprayed with butter-flavored cooking spray, sauté turkey and ham for 5 minutes or until lightly browned. In a large covered jar, combine chicken broth, dry milk powder, water, flour, and mustard. Shake well to blend. Pour broth mixture into skillet with meat. Add green beans. Mix well to combine. Bring mixture to a boil. Stir in rice and Cheddar cheese. Remove from heat, cover and let set for 5 minutes. Stir again just before serving.

HINT: If you don't have leftovers, purchase a chunk of cooked turkey breast from your local deli.

Each serving equals:

HE: 3 Protein • 1 Vegetable • ½ Bread • ¼ Skim Milk • 4 Optional Calories

197 Calories • 5 gm Fat • 27 gm Protein • 11 gm Carbohydrate • 722 mg Sodium • 1 gm Fiber

DIABETIC: 3 Meat • 1 Vegetable • 1 Starch

Applesauce Pork Balls

Many people are still surprised to find pork recipes in a book on healthy eating. Well, you're going to find many of my favorite dishes that feature lean pork, and why? Because people love the flavor, it's always been a festive food, and in moderation it's an ideal choice for a party. I think you'll enjoy the blend of applesauce and pork in this recipe, and you can easily freeze the leftovers—if there *are* any! ❍ Serves 8 (2 each)

> 16 ounces ground 90% lean pork
> 1 cup unsweetened applesauce☆
> 6 tablespoons (1½ ounces) dried fine bread crumbs
> 1 teaspoon dried parsley flakes
> 1¾ cups (one 15-ounce can) Hunt's Chunky Tomato Sauce
> ½ cup finely chopped onion
> 1 tablespoon Brown Sugar Twin

Preheat oven to 350 degrees. Spray an 8-by-8-inch baking dish with butter-flavored cooking spray. In a medium bowl, combine pork, ½ cup applesauce, bread crumbs, and parsley flakes. Form into 16 (1-inch) balls. Place balls in prepared baking dish. In a small bowl, combine tomato sauce, remaining ½ cup applesauce, onion, and Brown Sugar Twin. Pour tomato sauce mixture evenly over meatballs. Cover and bake for 45 minutes. Uncover and continue baking for 15 minutes. Place baking dish on a wire rack and let set for 5 minutes. When serving, evenly spoon sauce over meatballs.

Each serving equals:

HE: 1½ Protein • 1 Vegetable • ¼ Bread • ¼ Fruit •
1 Optional Calorie

---

123 Calories • 3 gm Fat • 14 gm Protein •
10 gm Carbohydrate • 429 mg Sodium • 1 gm Fiber

DIABETIC: 2 Meat • 1 Starch

Hawaiian Baked Pork Tenders

Ever been to a Hawaiian luau, where a whole roasted pig is often the centerpiece? That's kind of a difficult thing to reproduce for your backyard barbecue or tailgate party, but you can enjoy those same flavors in this islands-inspired dish! And I promise you, the cleanup is *much* easier. . . .   ❂ Serves 8

8 (4-ounce) lean pork cutlets or tenderloins
1¾ cups (one 15-ounce can) Hunt's Chunky Tomato Sauce
1 cup (one 8-ounce can) crushed pineapple, packed in fruit juice, undrained
½ cup chopped green bell pepper
2 tablespoons Brown Sugar Twin
¼ teaspoon dried minced garlic
⅛ teaspoon lemon pepper

Preheat oven to 350 degrees. Spray a 9-by-13-inch baking dish with butter-flavored cooking spray. In a large skillet sprayed with butter-flavored cooking spray, brown pork. Arrange browned pork in prepared baking dish. In a medium bowl, combine tomato sauce, undrained pineapple, green pepper, Brown Sugar Twin, garlic, and lemon pepper. Pour sauce mixture over meat. Cover and bake for 30 minutes. Uncover and continue baking for 15 minutes.

HINT: Don't overbrown pork or it will become tough.

Each serving equals:

HE: 3 Protein • 1 Vegetable • ¼ Fruit •
1 Optional Calorie

196 Calories • 4 gm Fat • 25 gm Protein •
15 gm Carbohydrate • 424 mg Sodium • 1 gm Fiber

DIABETIC: 3 Meat • 1 Vegetable • ½ Fruit or
3 Meat • 1 Carbohydrate

Baked Pork in Cider Gravy

After tasting this succulent dish, I think you'll agree with me that some food marriages, like pork and apples, are made in culinary heaven! This unusual way with pork tenderloins is so good, you won't wait for a party to prepare it! ● Serves 8

8 (4-ounce) lean pork cutlets
 or tenderloins
½ cup chopped onion
1 cup peeled and coarsely
 chopped fresh tomatoes
1 cup chopped celery
2 cups (4 small) cored, peeled,
 and sliced cooking apples

½ cup sliced fresh mushrooms
2 cups unsweetened apple juice
6 tablespoons all-purpose flour
⅛ teaspoon black pepper
2 tablespoons chopped fresh
 parsley or 2 teaspoons
 dried parsley flakes

Preheat oven to 350 degrees. Spray a 9-by-13-inch baking dish with butter-flavored cooking spray. In a large skillet sprayed with butter-flavored cooking spray, brown cutlets for about 3 minutes on each side. Place browned meat in prepared baking dish. In same skillet, combine onion, tomatoes, celery, apples, and mushrooms. Sauté for 5 minutes, stirring occasionally. In a covered jar, combine apple juice and flour. Shake well to blend. Add juice mixture to vegetable mixture. Mix well to combine. Bring mixture to a boil, stirring often. Stir in black pepper and parsley. Evenly spoon mixture over browned meat. Cover and bake for 45 minutes. Uncover and continue baking for 15 minutes. When serving, evenly spoon sauce over meat.

HINT: Don't overbrown pork or it will become tough.

Each serving equals:

HE: 3 Protein • ¾ Vegetable • 1 Fruit • ¼ Bread

122 Calories • 2 gm Fat • 7 gm Protein •
19 gm Carbohydrate • 36 mg Sodium • 1 gm Fiber

DIABETIC: 3 Meat • 1 Fruit • ½ Vegetable • ½ Starch

Grande Stuffed Baked Tomatoes

Most people expect a cold salad served in a wedge-cut tomato, so this recipe might be a revelation! The spicy filling tastes extra-special, and the flavors blend beautifully. If you've got an abundance of ripe tomatoes, this recipe is a knockout! ☉ Serves 8

16 ounces ground 90% lean turkey or beef
8 fresh medium-sized ripe tomatoes
1 cup chunky salsa (mild, medium, or hot)
⅓ cup Kraft fat-free mayonnaise
⅓ cup (1½ ounces) shredded Kraft reduced-fat Cheddar cheese

Preheat oven to 375 degrees. In a large skillet sprayed with olive oil–flavored cooking spray, brown meat. Place skillet on a wire rack and allow to cool completely. Split each tomato into 4 wedges, but DO NOT cut all the way to the bottom. Arrange tomatoes in a 9-by-13-inch baking dish. In a medium bowl, combine cooled meat and salsa. Stir in mayonnaise. Evenly stuff tomatoes with meat mixture. Sprinkle full ½ tablespoon Cheddar cheese over top of each. Bake for 20 to 25 minutes. Place baking dish on a wire rack and let set for 5 minutes.

Each serving equals:

HE: 1¾ Protein • 1¼ Vegetable • 7 Optional Calories

134 Calories • 6 gm Fat • 12 gm Protein •
8 gm Carbohydrate • 285 mg Sodium • 1 gm Fiber

DIABETIC: 2 Vegetable • 1½ Meat

He-Man Open-Faced Hoagies

In Iowa, they're known as hoagies, but anywhere they're consumed, they're called delicious! This cousin of Sloppy Joes is so easy, your teenagers will probably make this recipe their own.

● Serves 8 (2 each)

> 16 ounces ground 90% lean turkey or beef
>
> ½ cup chopped onion
>
> ½ cup chopped green bell pepper
>
> ½ cup (one 2.5-ounce jar) sliced mushrooms, drained
>
> 1¾ cups (one 15-ounce can) Hunt's Chunky Tomato Sauce
>
> 2 teaspoons Italian seasoning
>
> 8 reduced-calorie hamburger buns, halved
>
> 4 (¾-ounce) slices Kraft reduced-fat Cheddar cheese

Preheat oven to 375 degrees. In a large skillet sprayed with olive oil–flavored cooking spray, brown meat, onion, and green pepper. Add mushrooms, tomato sauce, and Italian seasoning. Mix well to combine. Lower heat and simmer for 10 minutes, stirring occasionally. Place bun halves on 2 cookie sheets. Spoon about ¼ cup meat sauce on each half. Cut Cheddar cheese slices in half diagonally and evenly arrange cheese halves over meat sauce. Bake for 15 minutes or until cheese is bubbly. Serve hot.

Each serving equals:

HE: 2 Protein • 1¼ Vegetable • 1 Bread

---

211 Calories • 7 gm Fat • 17 gm Protein •
20 gm Carbohydrate • 749 mg Sodium • 1 gm Fiber

DIABETIC: 2 Meat • 1 Vegetable • 1 Starch

Sauerkraut Pizza

Not everyone loves sauerkraut as much as Cliff and I do, but you'll find that including that tangy ingredient in this freshly homemade pizza recipe will be a real conversation-starter! With its blend of cheeses and its surprising sauerkraut crust, this dish is a real winner.

○ Serves 8

16 ounces ground 90% lean turkey or beef

2 cups (one 16-ounce can) sauerkraut, well drained

1¾ cups (one 15-ounce can) Hunt's Chunky Tomato Sauce

1 teaspoon Italian seasoning

1 tablespoon Brown Sugar Twin

½ cup (one 2.5-ounce jar) sliced mushrooms, drained

½ cup sliced onion

½ cup chopped green bell pepper

¾ cup (3 ounces) shredded Kraft reduced-fat mozzarella cheese

¾ cup (3 ounces) shredded Kraft reduced-fat Cheddar cheese

Preheat oven to 425 degrees. Spray a 9-by-13-inch baking dish with butter-flavored cooking spray. In a large skillet sprayed with butter-flavored cooking spray, brown meat. Layer sauerkraut in bottom of prepared baking dish. Sprinkle browned meat evenly over sauerkraut. In a medium bowl, combine tomato sauce, Italian seasoning, and Brown Sugar Twin. Pour sauce mixture evenly over meat. Evenly arrange mushrooms, onion, and green pepper over sauce. Layer mozzarella and Cheddar cheese evenly over vegetables. Bake for 20 to 25 minutes. Place baking dish on a wire rack and let set for 5 minutes. Divide into 8 servings.

Each serving equals:

HE: 2½ Protein • 1¾ Vegetable • 1 Optional Calorie

184 Calories • 8 gm Fat • 18 gm Protein •
10 gm Carbohydrate • 936 mg Sodium • 3 gm Fiber

DIABETIC: 2½ Meat • 2 Vegetable

Chop Suey Pasta Hot Dish

Chop suey actually means "odds and ends" in Chinese, so it's a perfect name for this blend of ingredients. I love casserole dishes like this one, because they look and smell so great coming from the oven, and you hardly fussed at all. ❂ Serves 8

16 ounces ground 90% lean turkey or beef

1½ cups chopped celery

1 cup chopped green bell pepper

½ cup chopped onion

1 (10¾-ounce) can Healthy Request Tomato Soup

1 tablespoon reduced-sodium soy sauce

¼ teaspoon black pepper

3 cups cooked elbow macaroni, rinsed and drained

¾ cup (3 ounces) shredded Kraft reduced-fat Cheddar cheese☆

Preheat oven to 350 degrees. Spray a 9-by-13-inch baking dish with butter-flavored cooking spray. In a large skillet sprayed with butter-flavored cooking spray, brown meat, celery, green pepper, and onion. Stir in tomato soup, soy sauce, and black pepper. Add macaroni and ¼ cup Cheddar cheese. Mix well to combine. Pour mixture into prepared baking dish. Evenly sprinkle remaining ½ cup Cheddar cheese over top. Bake for 25 or 30 minutes. Place baking dish on a wire rack and let set for 5 minutes. Divide into 8 servings.

HINT: 2 cups uncooked macaroni usually cooks to about 3 cups.

Each serving equals:

HE: 2 Protein • ¾ Bread • ¾ Vegetable • ¼ Slider • 3 Optional Calories

---

224 Calories • 7 gm Fat • 16 gm Protein • 24 gm Carbohydrate • 309 mg Sodium • 1 gm Fiber

---

DIABETIC: 2 Meat • 1 Starch • 1 Vegetable

Skillet Hamburger Celery Stroganoff

Most stroganoff recipes echo the creamy flavors of the Russian original, but I decided to perk this one up with the crunch of celery. Your guests may have trouble believing that any dish this rich could be prepared with low-fat ingredients, so don't be surprised to find them in the kitchen checking out the empty containers!

◐ Serves 8 (1 full cup)

16 ounces ground 90% lean turkey or beef
1 cup chopped onion
1 cup chopped celery
1 (10¾-ounce) can Healthy Request Cream of Celery Soup
⅓ cup skim milk
¼ teaspoon black pepper
1 cup (two 2.5-ounce jars) sliced mushrooms, undrained
4 cups hot cooked noodles, rinsed and drained
¾ cup Land O Lakes no-fat sour cream
2 teaspoons dried parsley flakes

In a large skillet sprayed with butter-flavored cooking spray, brown meat, onion, and celery. Stir in celery soup, skim milk, and black pepper. Add mushrooms and noodles. Mix well to combine. Lower heat and simmer for 10 minutes, stirring occasionally. Gently stir in sour cream and parsley flakes. Serve at once.

HINT: 3½ cups uncooked noodles usually cooks to about 4 cups.

Each serving equals:

HE: 1½ Protein • 1 Bread • ¾ Vegetable • ½ Slider • 3 Optional Calories

251 Calories • 7 gm Fat • 17 gm Protein • 30 gm Carbohydrate • 349 mg Sodium • 2 gm Fiber

DIABETIC: 2 Starch • 1½ Meat *or* 2 Carbohydrate

Grande Mexican Lasagna

Okay, okay, I know that probably no one in Mexico actually serves a true lasagna, but you'll be pleased and a little amazed at just how the tortillas take the place of wide lasagna noodles in this delectable dish. The flavor is so full-bodied, I had to call it "grande"!

❍ Serves 8

> 16 ounces ground 90% lean turkey or beef
> ¾ cup chopped onion
> 1¾ cups (one 14½-ounce can) Mexican stewed tomatoes,
>   coarsely chopped and undrained
> 1¾ cups (one 15-ounce can) Hunt's Chunky Tomato Sauce
> ¾ cup water
> 1 tablespoon taco seasoning
> 8 (6-inch) corn tortillas
> ¾ cup (3 ounces) shredded Kraft reduced-fat Cheddar cheese

Preheat oven to 350 degrees. Spray a 9-by-13-inch baking dish with olive oil–flavored cooking spray. In a large skillet sprayed with butter-flavored cooking spray, brown meat and onion. Add undrained stewed tomatoes, tomato sauce, and water. Mix well to combine. Stir in taco seasoning. Place a thin layer of meat mixture on bottom of prepared baking dish. Top with 4 tortillas. Turn to fit. Spread half of remaining sauce over top. Sprinkle half of Cheddar cheese over sauce. Layer 4 more tortillas over cheese. Turn to fit. Spread remaining sauce over tortillas. Sprinkle remaining Cheddar cheese over top. Bake for 30 minutes. Place baking dish on a wire rack and let set for 5 minutes. Cut into 8 servings.

Each serving equals:

> HE: 1½ Vegetable • 2 Protein • 1 Bread
> ───────────────────────────────────
> 175 Calories • 7 gm Fat • 14 gm Protein •
> 14 gm Carbohydrate • 296 mg Sodium • 0 gm Fiber
> ───────────────────────────────────
> DIABETIC: 2 Vegetable • 2 Meat • 1 Starch

Frankfurter Spanish Rice

If you're feeding a crowd of kids, you may want to add to your repertoire of dishes featuring one of their favorite foods: frankfurters! This recipe is simple to fix and great to serve just about anytime you've got lots of mouths to feed. ❂ Serves 8 (1 cup)

16 ounces Healthy Choice 97% fat-free frankfurters, diced
1 cup chopped onion
1 cup chopped green bell pepper
1¾ cups (one 15-ounce can) Hunt's Chunky Tomato Sauce
½ cup chunky salsa (mild, medium, or hot)
1 cup water
1⅓ cups (4 ounces) uncooked instant rice
1 tablespoon Brown Sugar Twin
1 teaspoon dried parsley flakes
1 teaspoon black pepper

In a large skillet sprayed with olive oil–flavored cooking spray, sauté frankfurters, onion, and green pepper for 5 minutes or until tender. Stir in tomato sauce, salsa, and water. Bring mixture to a boil. Add uncooked rice, Brown Sugar Twin, parsley flakes, and black pepper. Mix well to combine. Remove from heat, cover and let set for 5 minutes. Stir again just before serving.

Each serving equals:

HE: 1⅓ Protein • 1½ Vegetable • ½ Bread •
1 Optional Calorie

113 Calories • 1 gm Fat • 9 gm Protein •
17 gm Carbohydrate • 982 mg Sodium • 1 gm Fiber

DIABETIC: 1½ Meat • 1½ Vegetable • 1 Starch

Rio Taco Pie

Everybody loves tacos, but they can sometimes be messy eating as part of a buffet. I took all those irresistible flavors and combined them in this easy-to-fix pie, so serving is a breeze. Remember the preferences of your guests when choosing the salsa heat, and consider offering small bowls of hotter versions for courageous guests to spoon on top! ● Serves 8

8 ounces ground 90% lean turkey or beef

½ cup chopped onion

1¾ cups (one 15-ounce can) Hunt's Chunky Tomato Sauce

½ cup chunky salsa (mild, medium, or hot)

1 tablespoon taco seasoning

1 (8-ounce) can Pillsbury refrigerated crescent dinner rolls

¾ cup (3 ounces) shredded Kraft reduced-fat Cheddar cheese

1 cup shredded lettuce

¼ cup (1 ounce) sliced ripe olives

½ cup chopped fresh tomato

Preheat oven to 375 degrees. Spray a rimmed 9-by-13-inch cookie sheet with olive oil–flavored cooking spray. In a large skillet sprayed with butter-flavored cooking spray, brown meat and onion. Stir in tomato sauce, salsa, and taco seasoning. Lower heat and simmer for 5 minutes. Meanwhile, gently pat rolls into prepared cookie sheet, being sure to seal perforations. Prick bottom and sides with tines of a fork. Bake for 5 minutes. Evenly spoon meat sauce over partially baked crust. Sprinkle Cheddar cheese evenly over top. Continue baking for 5 minutes until cheese starts to melt. Place cookie sheet on a wire rack and let set for 5 minutes. Top with lettuce, olives, and tomato. Cut into 8 servings.

HINT: Good served with no-fat sour cream. If using, count optional calories accordingly.

Each serving equals:
HE: 2 Protein • 1½ Vegetable • 1 Bread •
5 Optional Calories

189 Calories • 9 gm Fat • 11 gm Protein •
16 gm Carbohydrate • 818 mg Sodium • 0 gm Fiber

DIABETIC: 2 Meat • 1 Vegetable • 1 Starch

Festive Ham Salad Buns

In my family, ham salad is a picnic and family reunion regular, so
I had to include a recipe for this old-fashioned favorite in this book.
Just be prepared with full platters, because everyone will surely grab
a bun!   ● Serves 8

1½ cups (9 ounces) finely diced   ¾ cup Kraft fat-free mayonnaise
    Dubuque 97% fat-free ham   ⅛ teaspoon black pepper
    or any extra-lean ham   1 cup finely shredded lettuce
2 hard-boiled eggs, diced   8 reduced-calorie hamburger
2 tablespoons diced pimientos   buns
¼ cup hot dog pickle relish

    In a medium bowl, combine ham, eggs, and pimientos. Add
pickle relish, mayonnaise, and black pepper. Mix well to combine.
Refrigerate for at least 30 minutes. Just before serving, stir lettuce
into ham mixture. For each sandwich, spoon about ½ cup mixture
between a hamburger bun.

Each serving equals:
HE: 1 Protein (¼ limited) • 1 Bread • ¼ Vegetable •
¼ Slider • 3 Optional Calories

147 Calories • 3 gm Fat • 9 gm Protein •
21 gm Carbohydrate • 659 mg Sodium • 0 gm Fiber

DIABETIC: 1½ Starch • 1 Meat

Buffet Baked Ham Salad

If you've got leftovers after a holiday ham, or you're simply looking for a satisfying entree for your next club meeting, this hot salad could be just the ticket! It delivers lots of good nutrition for very few calories and fat grams per serving, so it'll appeal to everyone from 3 to 93! ☻ Serves 8

3 full cups (18 ounces) finely
    diced Dubuque 97%
    fat-free ham or any
    extra-lean ham
2 cups finely diced celery
1½ cups Kraft fat-free
    mayonnaise
1 tablespoon dried onion flakes
2 teaspoons dried parsley
    flakes
1 tablespoon lemon juice

⅛ teaspoon black pepper
1 tablespoon prepared
    mustard
¼ cup canned chopped
    pimientos
2 hard-boiled eggs, sliced
20 Ritz Reduced Fat Crackers,
    made into crumbs
⅓ cup (1½ ounces) shredded
    Kraft reduced-fat Cheddar
    cheese

Preheat oven to 400 degrees. Spray a 9-by-13-inch baking dish with butter-flavored cooking spray. In a large bowl, combine ham and celery. Add mayonnaise, onion flakes, parsley flakes, lemon juice, black pepper, and mustard. Mix well to combine. Stir in pimientos and eggs. Spread mixture into prepared baking dish. In a medium bowl, combine cracker crumbs and Cheddar cheese. Evenly sprinkle mixture over top. Bake for 35 to 40 minutes. Place baking dish on a wire rack and let set for 5 minutes. Divide into 8 servings.

Each serving equals:

HE: 2 Protein (¼ limited) • ½ Vegetable • ½ Bread • ¼ Slider • 10 Optional Calories

170 Calories • 6 gm Fat • 14 gm Protein • 15 gm Carbohydrate • 856 mg Sodium • 1 gm Fiber

DIABETIC: 2 Meat • 1 Starch *or* Carbohydrate

Hawaiian Ham Sandwiches

I think ham and pineapple make wonderful "dance partners," don't you? Combined with a scrumptious dressing, those two lend their special magic to these delectable sandwiches. ☻ Serves 8

1 (8-ounce) package Philadelphia fat-free cream cheese

½ cup Kraft fat-free mayonnaise

2 teaspoons prepared mustard

2 tablespoons Brown Sugar Twin

2 cups (two 8-ounce cans) crushed pineapple, packed in fruit
    juice, drained, and ¼ cup liquid reserved

2 full cups (12 ounces) finely diced Dubuque 97% fat-free ham or
    any extra-lean ham

16 slices reduced-calorie wheat or oatmeal bread

1 cup finely shredded lettuce

In a large bowl, stir cream cheese with a spoon until soft. Stir in mayonnaise, mustard, Brown Sugar Twin, and reserved pineapple juice. Add ham and pineapple. Mix well to combine. For each sandwich, spread ½ cup ham filling on a slice of bread, sprinkle 2 tablespoons lettuce over filling and top with another slice of bread.

Each serving equals:

HE: 1½ Protein • 1 Bread • ½ Fruit • ¼ Vegetable •
11 Optional Calories

198 Calories • 2 gm Fat • 17 gm Protein •
28 gm Carbohydrate • 832 mg Sodium • 0 gm Fiber

DIABETIC: 2 Meat • 1 Starch • 1 Fruit or
2 Meat • 2 Carbohydrate

Pasta with Carrots and Ham

This is sort of a ham tetrazzini, I'd say, but made even more delicious by the addition of carrots and tangy cheese. It's a wonderful choice for a big buffet party because it doesn't lose its "oomph" too quickly sitting on the platter! ◐ Serves 8 (1 cup)

> 2 cups sliced fresh carrots
> 1 cup hot water
> 1½ cups (9 ounces) finely diced Dubuque 97% fat-free ham or any extra-lean ham
> 1 (10¾-ounce) can Healthy Request Cream of Celery Soup
> ⅔ cup Carnation Nonfat Dry Milk Powder
> 1 cup water
> ⅓ cup (1½ ounces) shredded Kraft reduced-fat Cheddar cheese
> 2 tablespoons chopped fresh parsley or 2 teaspoons dried parsley flakes
> ⅛ teaspoon black pepper
> 4 cups hot cooked spaghetti, rinsed and drained

In a large saucepan, cook carrots in water for about 10 minutes or until just tender. Drain. Meanwhile, in a large skillet sprayed with butter-flavored cooking spray, sauté ham for 5 minutes. Stir in celery soup, dry milk powder, water, Cheddar cheese, parsley, and black pepper. Add spaghetti and drained carrots. Mix well to combine. Lower heat and simmer for 8 to 10 minutes, stirring occasionally.

HINT: 3 cups uncooked spaghetti usually cooks to 4 cups.

Each serving equals:

HE: 1 Bread • 1 Protein • ½ Vegetable • ¼ Skim Milk • ¼ Slider • 1 Optional Calorie

---

199 Calories • 3 gm Fat • 13 gm Protein •
30 gm Carbohydrate • 512 mg Sodium • 2 gm Fiber

DIABETIC: 1½ Starch • 1 Meat • ½ Vegetable

Italian Ham Rotini

This recipe is a real melange of flavors, but they hold hands beautifully in this luscious casserole! If you haven't yet tried a reduced-fat Swiss cheese, I think you'll be pleasantly surprised at how much flavor it imparts to a baked dish like this one.

● Serves 8

> 2 full cups (12 ounces) diced Dubuque 97% fat-free ham or any
>   extra-lean ham
>
> 1¾ cups (one 15-ounce can) Hunt's Chunky Tomato Sauce
>
> 1 (10¾-ounce) can Healthy Request Tomato Soup
>
> ½ cup (one 2.5-ounce jar) sliced mushrooms, undrained
>
> 2 teaspoons Italian seasoning
>
> ¼ teaspoon black pepper
>
> 4 cups hot cooked rotini pasta, rinsed and drained
>
> 4 (¾-ounce) slices Kraft reduced-fat Swiss cheese, shredded

Preheat oven to 350 degrees. Spray a 9-by-13-inch baking dish with olive oil–flavored cooking spray. In a large skillet sprayed with olive oil–flavored cooking spray, sauté ham until browned. Add tomato sauce, tomato soup, undrained mushrooms, Italian seasoning, and black pepper. Mix well to combine. Lower heat and simmer for 15 minutes, stirring occasionally. Stir in rotini pasta. Spread mixture into prepared baking dish. Evenly sprinkle Swiss cheese over top. Bake for 25 to 30 minutes. Place baking dish on a wire rack and let set for 5 minutes. Divide into 8 servings.

HINT: 3 cups uncooked rotini pasta usually cooks to about 4 cups.

Each serving equals:

HE: 1½ Protein • 1 Bread • 1 Vegetable • ¼ Slider • 3 Optional Calories

---

191 Calories • 3 gm Fat • 12 gm Protein •
29 gm Carbohydrate • 904 mg Sodium • 3 gm Fiber

DIABETIC: 1½ Meat • 1½ Starch • 1 Vegetable

Amoré Ham and Cheese Pie

If you want to show people how much you love them, you couldn't do better than serve this pie inspired by the Italian word for love! In fact, by providing a healthy entree that sizzles with three different kinds of cheese, you're showing them just how well they can eat and still take good care of themselves! ● Serves 8

1 (8-ounce) can Pillsbury refrigerated crescent dinner rolls

1 egg, slightly beaten, or equivalent in egg substitute

¼ cup skim milk

¼ cup (¾ ounce) grated Kraft fat-free Parmesan cheese

⅛ teaspoon black pepper

1 teaspoon Italian seasoning

1 full cup (6 ounces) diced Dubuque 97% fat-free ham or any extra-lean ham

⅓ cup (1½ ounces) shredded Kraft reduced-fat Cheddar cheese

⅓ cup (1½ ounces) shredded Kraft reduced-fat mozzarella cheese

Preheat oven to 325 degrees. Spray a 9-inch pie plate with butter-flavored cooking spray. Unroll crescent rolls and separate dough into 8 triangles. Place 6 triangles into prepared pie plate, pressing pieces together to form a crust. In a large mixing bowl, combine egg, skim milk, Parmesan cheese, black pepper, and Italian seasoning. Add ham, Cheddar cheese, and mozzarella cheese. Mix well to combine. Pour mixture into pie plate. Roll out remaining 2 triangles flat. Cut into ½-inch strips. Crisscross strips over filling to form a lattice top. Bake for 35 to 40 minutes or until filling is set. Do not overbake. Place pie plate on a wire rack and let set for 5 minutes. Cut into 8 servings.

Each serving equals:

HE: 1¼ Protein • 1 Bread • 3 Optional Calories

164 Calories • 8 gm Fat • 10 gm Protein •
13 gm Carbohydrate • 551 mg Sodium • 1 gm Fiber

DIABETIC: 1 Meat • 1 Starch • 1 Fat

Baked Ham with Island Sauce

Close your eyes and imagine the wonderful aroma of a baked ham studded with pineapple—*mmmmm!* Now you can give your guests that scrumptious flavor with much less work, and just as much rich taste. Try this recipe with different kinds of mustard until you find the one that truly pleases your palate.   ● Serves 8

> 8 (3-ounce) slices Dubuque 97% fat-free ham or any extra-lean ham
> 1 cup (one 8-ounce can) crushed pineapple, packed in fruit juice, undrained
> 3 tablespoons Brown Sugar Twin
> 1 tablespoon vinegar
> 1 tablespoon prepared mustard

Preheat oven to 350 degrees. Spray a rimmed 9-by-13-inch cookie sheet with butter-flavored cooking spray. Place ham slices on prepared pan. In a small bowl, combine undrained pineapple, Brown Sugar Twin, vinegar, and mustard. Evenly spoon about 1 tablespoon sauce mixture over each ham slice. Bake for 20 to 25 minutes.

HINT: A 3-ounce slice of ham is usually ⅓ inch thick.

Each serving equals:

HE: 2 Protein • ¼ Fruit • 2 Optional Calories

111 Calories • 3 gm Fat • 14 gm Protein •
7 gm Carbohydrate • 745 mg Sodium • 0 gm Fiber

DIABETIC: 1½ Meat • ½ Fruit

Glorious Endings

Just as the finale of a great musical celebrates all the excitement generated during the show, a party dessert should be a kind of culinary curtain call! Don't you love hearing that collective gasp when the pies, cakes, and puddings arrive from the kitchen to decorate your table and dazzle your guests? No matter how they've indulged in the luscious goodies presented earlier, everyone is looking forward to a special treat for dessert.

My specialty since I first created Healthy Exchanges has been "sinful-looking but sinless" desserts, and I've selected lots of favorites for this collection of dishes for entertaining. Most of my pies and cheesecakes serve eight, which already makes them the ideal size for sharing with guests. And all of my desserts stir up so fast you'll be free to spend the hours before your party decorating your house and choosing what to wear!

If you're expecting healthy desserts to be bland and boring, you'll be happily surprised to discover how delicious and delightful my healthy treats can be. Prepared with easy-to-find ingredients, using the best store-bought items, and full of rich flavor, the glorious endings I've chosen to please your palate will transform the way you think about dessert—and turn any party host into a star! Garnished with such "forbidden" goodies as nuts, chocolate chips, even caramel and chocolate syrups, these dishes are a true grand finale!

Glorious Endings

Peanut Butter Candy Drops   150

Chocolate Graham Treats   151

Fruit Melba Meringue Cups   152

Pistachio Delight   154

Fiesta Cherry Burritos   156

Pineapple Pecan Pudding Shortcake   158

Pumpkin-Pecan Crunch   160

Applesauce Spice Cake   162

Apple Chocolate Chip Snack Cake   163

Rhubarb Custard Pizza   164

Apple Dessert Bars   166

Frozen Lemon Yogurt Pie   168

Lime Chiffon Banana Pie   169

Crunchy Munchy Banana Party Pie   170

Cherry Cloud in the Sky Pie   171

Cherry Banana Cream Pie   172

Raspberry Almond Cream Pie   173

Aloha Dream Pie   174

Lemon Blueberry Cream Pie   175

Raisin Pecan Meringue Pie   176

Coconut Lemon Meringue Pie   178

Caramel Apple Cheesecake   180

Cherry Celebration Cheesecake   182

Peanut Butter Candy Drops

A bowl of these makes a wonderful addition to the dessert table at any holiday gathering, when everyone is willing to go a little wild in celebration. Won't they be pleased to know they can partake with just about zero guilt? I'm sure of it! ☻ Serves 8 (2 each)

> ¼ cup Peter Pan reduced-fat chunky peanut butter
> ⅔ cup Carnation Nonfat Dry Milk Powder
> ¼ cup Nestlé Quik sugar-free chocolate milk mix
> 1 teaspoon vanilla extract
> ½ cup water
> 1 cup (3 ounces) purchased cornflake crumbs
> ½ cup raisins

Line a large cookie sheet with waxed paper. In a medium bowl, combine peanut butter, dry milk powder, Nestlé Quik, vanilla extract, and water. Add cornflake crumbs and raisins. Mix gently to combine. Drop mixture by teaspoonfuls onto prepared cookie sheet to form 16 drops. Refrigerate for at least 30 minutes. Cover and refrigerate any leftovers.

HINT: To plump up raisins without "cooking," place in a glass measuring cup and microwave on HIGH for 20 seconds.

Each serving equals:

HE: ½ Protein • ½ Fat • ½ Bread • ½ Fruit •
¼ Skim Milk • 10 Optional Calories

115 Calories • 3 gm Fat • 5 gm Protein •
17 gm Carbohydrate • 186 mg Sodium • 0 gm Fiber

DIABETIC: 1 Starch • ½ Fat

Chocolate Graham Treats

Something magical happens when you stir up a pot of chocolate pudding, and when it's combined with vanilla and graham cracker crumbs, you've got a winning combination that says "Welcome!"

● Serves 8 (3 pieces)

> 1 (4-serving) package JELL-O sugar-free chocolate cook-and-
> serve pudding mix
> ⅔ cup Carnation Nonfat Dry Milk Powder
> 1 cup water
> 1 teaspoon vanilla extract
> 1 tablespoon + 1 teaspoon reduced-calorie margarine
> 1 cup purchased graham cracker crumbs or 16 (2½-inch)
> graham crackers, made into crumbs

In a medium saucepan, combine dry pudding mix, dry milk powder, and water. Cook over medium heat, stirring constantly with a wire whisk, until mixture thickens and just starts to boil. Remove from heat. Stir in vanilla extract and margarine. Blend in graham cracker crumbs. Pat mixture into an 8-by-8-inch dish. Cover and refrigerate for at least 1 hour. Cut into 24 squares. Refrigerate any leftovers.

Each serving equals:

HE: ⅔ Bread • ¼ Fat • ¼ Skim Milk •
12 Optional Calories

---

102 Calories • 2 gm Fat • 3 gm Protein •
18 gm Carbohydrate • 185 mg Sodium • 0 gm Fiber

DIABETIC: 1 Starch

Fruit Melba Meringue Cups

Even if you've never dared make a lemon meringue pie, this recipe can turn you into a dessert chef extraordinaire! Just follow my simple instructions to produce a dish of such yummy flavor and lovely color, and you're bound to be asked for your "secret"!

◑ Serves 8

> 2 (4-serving) packages JELL-O sugar-free vanilla cook-and-serve pudding mix
>
> 4 cups (two 16-ounce cans) sliced peaches, packed in fruit juice, drained, and ½ cup liquid reserved
>
> 1½ cups water
>
> 2 tablespoons Brown Sugar Twin
>
> 1 teaspoon ground cinnamon
>
> 1½ cups fresh red raspberries
>
> 12 egg whites
>
> 1 cup Sugar Twin or Sprinkle Sweet
>
> 1½ teaspoons vanilla extract

Preheat oven to 425 degrees. In a large saucepan, combine dry pudding mix, reserved peach liquid, water, Brown Sugar Twin, and cinnamon. Cook over medium heat, stirring often with a wire whisk, until mixture thickens and starts to boil. Add peaches and raspberries. Mix gently just to combine. Evenly spoon fruit mixture into 8 (8-ounce) custard cups. In a large bowl, beat egg whites with an electric mixer until soft peaks form. Add Sugar Twin and vanilla extract. Continue beating until stiff peaks form. Spread meringue mixture evenly over top of each custard cup, being sure to seal to edges. Bake for 5 minutes or until meringue starts to turn brown. Place custard cups on a wire rack and allow to cool for at least 5 minutes.

HINT: Egg whites beat best at room temperature.

Each serving equals:

HE: 1¼ Fruit • ½ Protein • ¼ Slider •
3 Optional Calories

132 Calories • 0 gm Fat • 7 gm Protein •
26 gm Carbohydrate • 149 mg Sodium • 2 gm Fiber

DIABETIC: 1½ Fruit • ½ Meat

Pistachio Delight

I always keep a supply of pistachio pudding on hand so I can whip up this beautiful and tasty dessert. It joins so many delectable flavors in a symphony of sweet surprises, it'll be the hit of any meal it concludes!　　●　Serves 8

12 (2½-inch) graham cracker squares

¾ cup Yoplait plain fat-free yogurt

1⅔ cups Carnation Nonfat Dry Milk Powder☆

1½ teaspoons coconut extract

2 tablespoons Sugar Twin or Sprinkle Sweet

1 cup Cool Whip Lite

1 (8-ounce) package Philadelphia fat-free cream cheese

2 (4-serving) packages JELL-O sugar-free instant pistachio
    pudding mix

2 cups water

1 cup (one 8-ounce can) crushed pineapple, packed in fruit juice,
    undrained

2 tablespoons flaked coconut

Spray a 9-by-13-inch cake pan with butter-flavored cooking spray. Evenly arrange graham crackers in prepared cake pan. In a medium bowl, combine yogurt and ⅓ cup dry milk powder. Blend in coconut extract, Sugar Twin, and Cool Whip Lite. Set aside. In a large bowl, stir cream cheese with a spoon until soft. Blend in ¾ cup of the yogurt mixture. Spread mixture evenly over graham cracker crust. In a large bowl, combine dry pudding mixes, remaining 1⅓ cups dry milk powder, and water. Mix well using a wire whisk. Stir in undrained pineapple. Spread pudding mixture evenly over cream cheese layer. Refrigerate for 5 minutes. Evenly spread remaining yogurt mixture over set filling. Sprinkle coconut evenly over top. Refrigerate for at least 1 hour. Cut into 8 servings.

Each serving equals:

HE: ¾ Skim Milk • ½ Bread • ½ Protein • ¼ Fruit •
½ Slider • 10 Optional Calories

---

178 Calories • 2 gm Fat • 11 gm Protein •
29 gm Carbohydrate • 509 mg Sodium • 1 gm Fiber

DIABETIC: 1 Starch • 1 Skim Milk • ½ Meat

Fiesta Cherry Burritos

When I first began experimenting with tortillas as part of a sweet fruit dessert, everyone at my restaurant, JO's Kitchen Cafe, was more than pleased with the results! The color of this dish is part of its special charm, but the cinnamon is the secret extra that gives it a taste worthy of cheers! Olé!   ● Serves 8

1 (4-serving) package JELL-O sugar-free vanilla cook-and-serve
    pudding mix
¾ cup water
2 cups (one 16-ounce can) tart red cherries, packed in water,
    drained
2 to 3 drops red food coloring
½ teaspoon almond extract
8 (6-inch) flour tortillas
1 teaspoon ground cinnamon
2 tablespoons Sugar Twin or Sprinkle Sweet

Preheat oven to 350 degrees. Spray a large cookie sheet with butter-flavored cooking spray. In a medium saucepan, combine dry pudding mix and water. Stir in cherries. Cook over medium heat, stirring often, until mixture thickens and starts to boil, being careful not to crush cherries. Remove from heat. Add red food coloring and almond extract. Mix gently to combine. Evenly spoon about 3 tablespoons cherry filling in center of each tortilla. Fold one edge over filling and roll tightly to opposite side. Place seam side down on cookie sheet. Spray top of each tortilla with butter-flavored cooking spray. In a small bowl, combine cinnamon and Sugar Twin. Evenly sprinkle cinnamon mixture over tops of tortillas. Bake for 10 to 12 minutes. Good served hot or cold.

Each serving equals:

HE: 1 Bread • ½ Fruit • 12 Optional Calories

97 Calories • 1 gm Fat • 2 gm Protein •
20 gm Carbohydrate • 178 mg Sodium • 1 gm Fiber

DIABETIC: 1 Starch • ½ Fruit

Pineapple Pecan Pudding Shortcake

I should wear a T-shirt that says, "I'd like to sprinkle pecans on EVERYTHING!" It is my most favorite nut, and the perfect addition to this moist and delectable cake that looks as luscious as it tastes.

○ Serves 8

1½ cups Bisquick Reduced Fat Baking Mix

1 (4-serving) package JELL-O sugar-free instant vanilla pudding mix

2 cups (two 8-ounce cans) pineapple tidbits, packed in fruit juice, drained, and ½ cup liquid reserved

¼ cup (1 ounce) chopped pecans

⅓ cup skim milk

½ cup water

1 tablespoon + 1 teaspoon reduced-calorie margarine

2 tablespoons Brown Sugar Twin

¼ teaspoon ground cinnamon

Preheat oven to 375 degrees. Spray a 9-by-9-inch cake pan with butter-flavored cooking spray. In a large bowl, combine baking mix, dry pudding mix, pineapple, and pecans. Add skim milk. Mix well to combine. Spread batter into prepared baking dish. In a small saucepan, combine reserved pineapple liquid, water, margarine, Brown Sugar Twin, and cinnamon. Cook over medium heat, stirring constantly, until mixture just starts to boil. Pour hot mixture evenly over batter. Bake for 35 to 40 minutes or until a toothpick inserted in center comes out clean. Place baking dish on a wire rack and allow to cool. Cut into 8 servings.

HINTS: 1. If you can't find tidbits, use chunk pineapple and coarsely chop.

2. Good served warm with sugar and fat-free vanilla ice cream *or* cold with Cool Whip Lite. If using either, count optional calories accordingly.

Each serving equals:

HE: 1 Bread • ¾ Fat • ½ Fruit • 17 Optional Calories

173 Calories • 5 gm Fat • 3 gm Protein •
29 gm Carbohydrate • 427 mg Sodium • 1 gm Fiber

DIABETIC: 1 Starch • 1 Fat • ½ Fruit

Pumpkin-Pecan Crunch

Since pumpkin is available in cans all year long, there's no need to wait until the holidays to enjoy its unique flavor and texture. On the other hand, your guests at any holiday bash won't go home happy unless there's something cozy warm on the menu that features pumpkin! ○ Serves 8

21 (2½-inch) graham cracker squares☆
1 (4-serving) package JELL-O sugar-free vanilla cook-and-serve pudding mix
⅔ cup Carnation Nonfat Dry Milk Powder
1 cup water
2 cups (one 16-ounce can) pumpkin
2 teaspoons pumpkin pie spice
1 teaspoon vanilla extract
3 tablespoons Bisquick Reduced Fat Baking Mix
1 tablespoon + 1 teaspoon reduced-calorie margarine
¼ cup (1 ounce) chopped pecans

Preheat oven to 350 degrees. Spray a 9-by-13-inch cake pan with butter-flavored cooking spray. Evenly arrange 12 graham crackers in prepared cake pan. In a large saucepan, combine dry pudding mix, dry milk powder, and water. Stir in pumpkin and pumpkin pie spice. Cook over medium heat, stirring often until mixture thickens and starts to boil. Remove from heat. Stir in vanilla extract. Evenly spread pumpkin mixture over graham crackers. Crush remaining graham crackers. In a medium bowl, combine cracker crumbs, baking mix, and margarine. Mix with a fork until crumbly. Stir in pecans. Evenly sprinkle topping mixture over pumpkin mixture. Bake for 35 to 40 minutes. Place cake pan on a wire rack and allow to cool completely. Cut into 8 servings.

HINT: Good topped with 1 tablespoon Cool Whip Lite, but don't forget to count the few additional calories.

Each serving equals:

HE: 1 Fat • ½ Vegetable • ½ Bread • ¼ Skim Milk • ¼ Slider • 5 Optional Calories

177 Calories • 5 gm Fat • 7 gm Protein • 26 gm Carbohydrate • 377 mg Sodium • 1 gm Fiber

DIABETIC: 1½ Starch • 1 Fat

Applesauce Spice Cake

I tasted an applesauce-raisin tea cake once, then hurried home to invent my own healthy version of that delightful treat! Applesauce is a great substitute for shortening in many recipes, but here it's the star of the show, and it deserves lots of applause.

○ Serves 8

1½ cups all-purpose flour
½ cup Sugar Twin or
    Sprinkle Sweet
¼ teaspoon salt
1 teaspoon baking soda
2 teaspoons pumpkin
    pie spice

½ cup unsweetened applesauce
¾ cup water
1 tablespoon vinegar
2 teaspoons vanilla extract
6 tablespoons raisins

Preheat oven to 350 degrees. Spray a 9-by-9-inch cake pan with butter-flavored cooking spray. In a large bowl, combine flour, Sugar Twin, salt, baking soda, and pumpkin pie spice. In a small bowl, combine applesauce, water, vinegar, vanilla extract, and raisins. Add applesauce mixture to flour mixture. Mix gently to combine. Pour mixture into prepared cake pan. Bake for 20 to 25 minutes or until a toothpick inserted in center comes out clean. Place cake pan on a wire rack and allow to cool completely. Cut into 8 servings.

HINT: Good served with Cool Whip Lite, but don't forget to count the few additional calories.

Each serving equals:

HE: 1 Bread • ½ Fruit • 6 Optional Calories

120 Calories • 0 gm Fat • 3 gm Protein •
27 gm Carbohydrate • 229 mg Sodium • 1 gm Fiber

DIABETIC: 1 Starch • ½ Fruit

Apple Chocolate Chip Snack Cake

Mini chocolate chips have been one of the best "weapons" in my arsenal of healthy cooking secrets since I first began stirring up Healthy Exchanges recipes. The simple truth is that when you can taste some genuine chocolate flavor, even just a few chips per serving, you feel as if you're eating the real thing. Who would have thought that apples and chocolate chips would make such delicious partners?   ☺ Serves 8

> 1½ cups Bisquick Reduced Fat Baking Mix
> 1 (4-serving) package JELL-O sugar-free instant vanilla pudding mix
> ½ teaspoon apple pie spice
> 1½ cups unsweetened apple juice
> 1½ cups (3 small) cored, peeled, and diced cooking apples
> ⅓ cup (1½ ounces) mini chocolate chips

Preheat oven to 350 degrees. Spray a 9-by-9-inch cake pan with butter-flavored cooking spray. In a medium bowl, combine baking mix, dry pudding mix, and apple pie spice. Add apple juice. Mix well to combine. Stir in apples and chocolate chips. Spread batter into prepared cake pan. Bake for 40 to 45 minutes, or until a toothpick inserted in center comes out clean. Place cake pan on a wire rack and allow to cool completely. Cut into 8 servings.

Each serving equals:

HE: 1 Bread • ¾ Fruit • ½ Slider • 1 Optional Calorie

155 Calories • 3 gm Fat • 2 gm Protein •
30 gm Carbohydrate • 415 mg Sodium • 1 gm Fiber

DIABETIC: 1½ Starch • ½ Fruit *or*
2 Carbohydrate

Rhubarb Custard Pizza

If you grow up in Iowa, you just can't wait until those first stalks of rhubarb pop out of the ground or appear in the market! As soon as they do, you're inspired to stir up a favorite rhubarb recipe for your family and friends. Here's one that bakes up flaky light and oh-so-good! ☻ Serves 8

> 1 (8-ounce) can Pillsbury refrigerated crescent dinner rolls
> 1 (8-ounce) package Philadelphia fat-free cream cheese
> ½ teaspoon vanilla extract
> Sugar substitute to equal 1 tablespoon sugar
> 1 (4-serving) package JELL-O sugar-free vanilla cook-and-serve pudding mix
> ½ cup water
> 4 cups cut rhubarb

Preheat oven to 425 degrees. Spray a rimmed 9-by-13-inch cookie sheet with butter-flavored cooking spray. Gently pat rolls into prepared pan, being sure to seal perforations. Bake for 6 to 7 minutes or until light golden brown. Place cookie sheet on a wire rack and allow to cool. In a medium bowl, stir cream cheese with a spoon until soft. Add vanilla extract and sugar substitute. Mix well to combine. Spread mixture evenly over cooled crust. In a medium saucepan, combine pudding mix and water. Stir in rhubarb. Cook over medium heat, stirring often, until rhubarb is tender and sauce begins to thicken. Place pan on a wire rack and let cool 10 minutes. Spread rhubarb mixture evenly over cream cheese mixture. Cover and refrigerate for at least 1 hour. Cut into 8 servings.

HINT:　Good topped with 1 tablespoon Cool Whip Lite, but don't forget to count the few additional calories.

Each serving equals:

HE: 1 Bread • 1 Vegetable • ½ Protein •
11 Optional Calories

---

129 Calories • 5 gm Fat • 4 gm Protein •
17 gm Carbohydrate • 374 mg Sodium • 1 gm Fiber

DIABETIC: 1 Starch • 1 Fat

Apple Dessert Bars

Bar cookies are a great item to serve at any party—they're easy to eat with your fingers, and nobody frowns if you help yourself to two! These taste a little like a French apple pie, with the warm apples and raisins mingling deliciously with a layer of cream cheese. Yum!   ◐   Serves 8 (2 bars)

1 (8-ounce) can Pillsbury refrigerated crescent dinner rolls

1 (4-serving) package JELL-O sugar-free vanilla cook-and-serve pudding mix

1 (4-serving) package JELL-O sugar-free lemon gelatin

1⅓ cups water

3 cups (6 small) cored, unpeeled, and diced cooking apples

¼ cup raisins

1½ teaspoons ground cinnamon☆

1 (8-ounce) package Philadelphia fat-free cream cheese

Sugar substitute to equal 2 tablespoons sugar

Preheat oven to 425 degrees. Spray a rimmed 9-by-13-inch cookie sheet with butter-flavored cooking spray. Gently pat rolls into prepared cookie sheet, being sure to seal perforations. Bake for

6 to 8 minutes or until light golden brown. Place cookie sheet on a wire rack and allow to cool. In a medium saucepan, combine dry pudding mix, dry gelatin, and water. Add apples, raisins, and 1 teaspoon cinnamon. Mix well to combine. Cook over medium heat, stirring often, until mixture thickens and starts to boil. Remove from heat. Place saucepan on a wire rack and allow to cool for 15 minutes. Meanwhile, in a medium bowl, stir cream cheese with a spoon until soft. Add sugar substitute and remaining ½ teaspoon cinnamon. Mix gently to combine. Spread cream cheese mixture evenly over cooled crust. Spread cooled apple mixture evenly over cream cheese layer. Refrigerate for about 2 hours. Cut into 16 bars.

HINT: DO NOT use inexpensive rolls. They don't cover the pan properly.

Each serving equals:

HE: 1 Bread • 1 Fruit • ½ Protein • 16 Optional Calories

173 Calories • 5 gm Fat • 7 gm Protein •
25 gm Carbohydrate • 485 mg Sodium • 1 gm Fiber

DIABETIC: 1 Starch • 1 Fruit • ½ Meat • ½ Fat

Frozen Lemon Yogurt Pie

Instead of picking up a pricey prepared dessert filled with excess sugar and fat, why not stir up this super-speedy frozen pie that just sings out its lemony flavor with every bite? Just remember to give it time to thaw before your guests dig in their forks!

⊙ Serves 8

> 3 cups Yoplait plain fat-free yogurt
> 1 cup Cool Whip Lite
> 2 (4-serving) packages JELL-O sugar-free lemon gelatin
> 1 (6-ounce) Keebler shortbread piecrust

In a large bowl, combine yogurt and Cool Whip Lite. Blend in dry gelatin. Mix well using a wire whisk. Spread yogurt mixture evenly into piecrust. Freeze for at least 4 hours. Remove from freezer 30 minutes before serving. Cut into 8 servings.

HINT: If you like your lemon less tart, stir in sugar substitute to equal 2 tablespoons sugar when adding dry gelatin.

Each serving equals:

HE: ½ Bread • ½ Skim Milk • ¾ Slider •
15 Optional Calories

---

190 Calories • 6 gm Fat • 8 gm Protein •
26 gm Carbohydrate • 249 mg Sodium • 1 gm Fiber

DIABETIC: 1 Starch • 1 Fat • ½ Skim Milk

Lime Chiffon Banana Pie

Cliff is a big fan of chiffon pies, those light and luscious desserts that melt in your mouth in an instant, but keep your tastebuds happy all day! This one looks pretty and tastes even better than it looks, so serve it for a summer card party and feel like the queen of hearts! ○ Serves 8

1 (4-serving) package JELL-O sugar-free vanilla cook-and-serve
    pudding mix
1 (4-serving) package JELL-O sugar-free lime gelatin
1½ cups water
2 teaspoons lime juice
1 cup Cool Whip Lite
2 cups (2 medium) sliced bananas
1 (6-ounce) Keebler graham cracker piecrust

In a medium saucepan, combine dry pudding mix, dry gelatin, and water. Cook over medium heat, stirring often, until mixture thickens and starts to boil. Remove from heat. Stir in lime juice. Place saucepan on a wire rack and allow to cool for 20 minutes, stirring occasionally. Gently fold in Cool Whip Lite. Layer bananas in bottom of piecrust. Spread cooled pudding mixture evenly over bananas. Refrigerate for at least 1 hour. Cut into 8 servings.

HINTS: To prevent bananas from turning brown, mix with 1 teaspoon lemon juice or sprinkle with Fruit Fresh.

Each serving equals:

HE: ½ Bread • ½ Fruit • 1 Slider • 5 Optional Calories

174 Calories • 6 gm Fat • 2 gm Protein •
28 gm Carbohydrate • 328 mg Sodium • 1 gm Fiber

DIABETIC: 1 Starch • 1 Fruit • 1 Fat

Crunchy Munchy Banana Party Pie

This is one of those recipes that just overflows with goodies and looks impossibly decadent! Imagine—chocolate syrup . . . pecans . . . chocolate chips . . . and whipped topping—how all those flavors will party hearty in your mouth!　　● Serves 8

1 (4-serving) package JELL-O
　　sugar-free instant
　　vanilla pudding mix
⅔ cup Carnation Nonfat
　　Dry Milk Powder
1⅓ cups water
¾ cup Cool Whip Lite ☆

2 tablespoons (½ ounce) mini
　　chocolate chips
2 tablespoons (½ ounce) chopped
　　pecans
2 cups (2 medium) diced bananas
1 (6-ounce) Keebler chocolate
　　piecrust
2 teaspoons chocolate syrup

In a large bowl, combine dry pudding mix, dry milk powder, and water. Mix well using a wire whisk. Blend in ¼ cup Cool Whip Lite. Add chocolate chips, pecans, and bananas. Mix gently to combine. Spread mixture evenly into piecrust. Refrigerate for 5 minutes. Spread remaining ½ cup Cool Whip Lite over set filling. Refrigerate for at least 1 hour. Cut into 8 servings. Just before serving, drizzle chocolate syrup evenly over top.

HINT: To prevent bananas from turning brown, mix with 1 teaspoon lemon juice or sprinkle with Fruit Fresh.

Each serving equals:

HE: ½ Bread • ½ Fruit • ¼ Skim Milk • ¼ Fat •
1 Slider • 9 Optional Calories

208 Calories • 8 gm Fat • 4 gm Protein •
30 gm Carbohydrate • 160 mg Sodium • 1 gm Fiber

DIABETIC: 1½ Starch • 1 Fat • ½ Fruit *or*
2 Carbohydrate • 1 Fat

Cherry Cloud in the Sky Pie

There's nothing more American than cherry pie, is there? And it would be downright unpatriotic not to include at least one scrumptious cherry pie recipe in this book of celebrations, so—here's my vote for a perfect "watch the fireworks" dessert!

○ Serves 8

> 1 (4-serving) package JELL-O sugar-free vanilla cook-and-serve
>   pudding mix
> 1 (4-serving) package JELL-O sugar-free cherry gelatin
> 2 cups (one 16-ounce can) tart red cherries, packed in water,
>   drained, and ½ cup liquid reserved

½ cup water

1 teaspoon almond extract

1 (8-ounce) package Philadelphia fat-free cream cheese

1 cup Cool Whip Lite

1 (6-ounce) Keebler graham cracker piecrust

In a medium saucepan, combine dry pudding mix, dry gelatin, reserved cherry liquid, and water. Stir in cherries. Cook over medium heat, stirring often, until mixture thickens and starts to boil, being careful not to crush cherries. Remove from heat. Stir in almond extract. Place pan on a wire rack and allow to cool completely. In a medium bowl, stir cream cheese with a spoon until soft. Blend in Cool Whip Lite. Add cream cheese mixture to cooled cherry mixture. Mix gently to combine. Spread mixture evenly into piecrust. Refrigerate for at least 2 hours. Cut into 8 servings.

Each serving equals:

HE: ½ Protein • ½ Bread • ½ Fruit • 1 Slider •
5 Optional Calories

---

182 Calories • 6 gm Fat • 6 gm Protein •
26 gm Carbohydrate • 501 mg Sodium • 1 gm Fiber

DIABETIC: 1 Starch • ½ Fruit • ½ Meat • ½ Fat

Cherry Banana Cream Pie

My kids have always loved banana cream pie, so I've had to be extra-inventive in coming up with variations on that beloved theme. Here's a version that combines lush color and cherry flavor with their favorite fruit. ● Serves 8

> 1 (4-serving) package JELL-O sugar-free instant vanilla pudding mix
>
> 1 (4-serving) package JELL-O sugar-free cherry gelatin
>
> ⅔ cup Carnation Nonfat Dry Milk Powder
>
> 1¼ cups water
>
> 1 cup Cool Whip Lite☆
>
> 1 (6-ounce) Keebler shortbread piecrust
>
> 2 cups (2 medium) sliced bananas
>
> 4 maraschino cherries, halved

In a large bowl, combine dry pudding mix, dry gelatin, and dry milk powder. Add water. Mix well using a wire whisk. Blend in ½ cup Cool Whip Lite. Spread ⅓ of mixture evenly over bottom of piecrust. Evenly layer bananas over top. Spread remaining pudding mixture evenly over bananas. Refrigerate for 5 minutes. Spread remaining ½ cup Cool Whip Lite evenly over set filling. Evenly garnish with maraschino cherry halves. Refrigerate for at least 1 hour. Cut into 8 servings.

HINT: To prevent bananas from turning brown, mix with 1 teaspoon lemon juice or sprinkle with Fruit Fresh.

Each serving equals:

HE: ½ Bread • ½ Fruit • ¼ Skim Milk • 1 Slider • 13 Optional Calories

202 Calories • 6 gm Fat • 4 gm Protein • 33 gm Carbohydrate • 318 mg Sodium • 1 gm Fiber

DIABETIC: 1 Starch • 1 Fruit • 1 Fat *or* 2 Carbohydrate • 1 Fat

Raspberry Almond Cream Pie

The season for fresh raspberries isn't very long, so we've got to be ready for those wonderful weeks when they appear in the grocery store. I think you'll quickly grow to love how the almonds embrace those pretty red jewels and sing a flavor duet in your mouth!

● Serves 8

1½ cups fresh red raspberries☆
1 (6-ounce) Keebler shortbread
    piecrust
1 (4-serving) package JELL-O
    sugar-free instant vanilla
    pudding mix
⅔ cup Carnation Nonfat Dry
    Milk Powder

1⅓ cups water
1 teaspoon almond extract☆
1 cup Cool Whip Lite☆
3 to 4 drops red food coloring
1 tablespoon (¼ ounce) chopped
    almonds

Reserve ¼ cup raspberries. Place remaining 1¼ cups raspberries in bottom of piecrust. In a large bowl, combine dry pudding mix, dry milk powder, and water. Mix well using a wire whisk. Blend in ½ teaspoon almond extract and ¼ cup Cool Whip Lite. Spread pudding mixture evenly over raspberries. Refrigerate while preparing topping. In a small bowl, combine remaining ¾ cup Cool Whip Lite, remaining ½ teaspoon almond extract, and red food coloring. Spread topping mixture evenly over set filling. Evenly sprinkle almonds and remaining ¼ cup raspberries over top. Refrigerate for at least 1 hour. Cut into 8 servings.

Each serving equals:

HE: ½ Bread • ¼ Fruit • ¼ Skim Milk • 1 Slider •
9 Optional Calories

170 Calories • 6 gm Fat • 3 gm Protein •
26 gm Carbohydrate • 291 mg Sodium • 1 gm Fiber

DIABETIC: 1 Starch • 1 Fruit • 1 Fat *or*
2 Carbohydrate • 1 Fat

Aloha Dream Pie

I love to close my eyes and think of soft Hawaiian breezes, especially when the temperature in DeWitt, Iowa, is below zero! Now you don't just have to dream about the islands—you can lose yourself in the sweet taste of this quick and easy pie. If you can't welcome your guests with leis of flowers, you can win their hearts with this enticing pie. ☺ Serves 8

2 cups (2 medium) diced bananas	1 cup (one 8-ounce can) crushed pineapple, packed in fruit juice, undrained
1 (6-ounce) Keebler graham cracker piecrust	
1 (4-serving) package JELL-O sugar-free instant butterscotch pudding mix	1 cup water
	¾ cup Cool Whip Lite
	¾ teaspoon coconut extract
⅔ cup Carnation Nonfat Dry Milk Powder	2 tablespoons flaked coconut

Place bananas in bottom of piecrust. In a medium bowl, combine dry pudding mix and dry milk powder. Add undrained pineapple and water. Mix well using a wire whisk. Spread pudding mixture evenly over bananas. Refrigerate while preparing topping. In a small bowl, combine Cool Whip Lite and coconut extract. Evenly spread topping mixture over set filling. Sprinkle coconut evenly over top. Refrigerate for at least 1 hour. Cut into 8 servings.

HINT: To prevent bananas from turning brown, mix with 1 teaspoon lemon juice or sprinkle with Fruit Fresh.

Each serving equals:

HE: ¾ Fruit • ½ Bread • ¼ Skim Milk • 1 Slider • 1 Optional Calorie

214 Calories • 6 gm Fat • 3 gm Protein • 37 gm Carbohydrate • 299 mg Sodium • 1 gm Fiber

DIABETIC: 1½ Starch • 1 Fruit • 1 Fat *or* 2½ Carbohydrate • 1 Fat

Lemon Blueberry Cream Pie

I've always thought that blueberries and lemon flavor go especially well together, and I've created other recipes that marry these two luscious tastes. The filling for this luxurious cream pie is especially pretty, and you'll want to serve it often! ☺ Serves 8

1 (4-serving) package JELL-O sugar-free lemon gelatin
1 (4-serving) package JELL-O sugar-free instant vanilla pudding
    mix
⅔ cup Carnation Nonfat Dry Milk Powder
1½ cups water
1 cup Cool Whip Lite ☆
1½ cups fresh blueberries
1 (6-ounce) Keebler shortbread piecrust

In a large bowl, combine dry gelatin, dry pudding mix, dry milk powder, and water. Mix well using a wire whisk. Blend in ¼ cup Cool Whip Lite. Gently stir in blueberries. Spread mixture evenly into piecrust. Refrigerate for 5 minutes. Spread remaining ¾ cup Cool Whip Lite over set filling. Refrigerate for at least 1 hour. Cut into 8 servings.

HINT: Do not use frozen blueberries. They are not firm enough for filling.

Each serving equals:

HE: ½ Bread • ¼ Fruit • ¼ Skim Milk • 1 Slider •
7 Optional Calories

182 Calories • 6 gm Fat • 4 gm Protein •
28 gm Carbohydrate • 255 mg Sodium • 2 gm Fiber

DIABETIC: 1 Starch • 1 Fruit • 1 Fat

Raisin Pecan Meringue Pie

I'm not sure if creamy raisin pies are more popular in the Midwest than anywhere else, but I do know that they're a mainstay of nearly every family reunion I've ever been to! Yes, it's a bit of extra work to pull out your electric mixer in order to whip the egg whites into frothy peaks, but you'll see that it's well worth the trouble. This pie could definitely compete for a prize at the state fair!

● Serves 8

> 1 Pillsbury refrigerated unbaked 9-inch piecrust
> 1 (4-serving) package JELL-O sugar-free vanilla cook-and-serve
> pudding mix
> ⅔ cup Carnation Nonfat Dry Milk Powder
> 1⅔ cups water
> 1 cup raisins
> 2 teaspoons vanilla extract☆
> ¼ cup (1 ounce) chopped pecans
> 6 egg whites
> ½ cup Sugar Twin or Sprinkle Sweet

Preheat oven to 450 degrees. Place piecrust in a 9-inch pie plate. Flute edges and prick bottom and sides with tines of a fork. Bake for 9 to 10 minutes. Place pie plate on a wire rack and allow to cool. Lower heat to 350 degrees. Meanwhile, in a medium saucepan, combine dry pudding mix, dry milk powder, and water. Stir in raisins. Cook over medium heat, stirring constantly with a wire whisk, until mixture thickens and starts to boil. Remove from heat. Stir in 1 teaspoon vanilla extract and pecans. Spread mixture evenly into baked piecrust. In a large bowl, beat egg whites with an electric mixer until soft peaks form. Add Sugar Twin and remaining 1 teaspoon vanilla extract. Continue beating until stiff peaks form. Spread meringue mixture evenly over filling mixture, being sure to seal to edges of piecrust. Bake for 5 to 6 minutes or until meringue starts to turn brown. Place pie plate on a wire rack and allow to cool completely. Cut into 8 servings.

HINTS: 1. Egg whites beat best at room temperature.

2. Meringue pie cuts easily if you dip a sharp knife in warm water before slicing.

Each serving equals:

HE: 1 Fruit • ½ Fat • ½ Bread • ¼ Protein •
¼ Skim Milk • ¾ Slider • 6 Optional Calories

241 Calories • 9 gm Fat • 6 gm Protein •
34 gm Carbohydrate • 340 mg Sodium • 1 gm Fiber

DIABETIC: 2 Fat • 1 Fruit • 1 Starch *or*
2 Fat • 2 Carbohydrate

Coconut Lemon Meringue Pie

This is a wonderful variation on that dessert classic, lemon meringue pie, made more delicious by the addition of coconut extract in the filling and flaked coconut on top! Isn't it great to serve a pie this yummy and know it's just over 150 calories per serving? That ought to be impossible, but with you in mind, I found a way!

● Serves 8

> 1 Pillsbury refrigerated unbaked 9-inch piecrust
>
> 2 (4-serving) packages JELL-O sugar-free vanilla cook-and-serve
>   pudding mix
>
> 1 (4-serving) package JELL-O sugar-free lemon gelatin
>
> 2½ cups water
>
> 1½ teaspoons coconut extract☆
>
> 6 egg whites
>
> ½ cup Sugar Twin or Sprinkle Sweet
>
> 2 tablespoons flaked coconut

Preheat oven to 450 degrees. Place piecrust in a 9-inch pie plate. Flute edges and prick bottom and sides with tines of a fork. Bake for 9 to 11 minutes or until lightly browned. Place pie plate on a wire rack and allow to cool completely. Lower heat to 350 degrees. Meanwhile, in a medium saucepan, combine dry pudding mixes and dry gelatin. Add water. Mix well to combine. Cook over medium heat, stirring often, until mixture thickens and starts to boil. Stir in 1 teaspoon coconut extract. Pour hot mixture into cooled piecrust. In a large bowl, beat egg whites with an electric mixer until soft peaks form. Add Sugar Twin and remaining ½ teaspoon coconut extract. Continue beating until stiff peaks form. Spread meringue mixture evenly over filling mixture, being sure to seal to edges of piecrust. Evenly sprinkle coconut over top. Bake for 10 to 15 minutes or until meringue starts to turn brown. Place pie plate on a wire rack and allow to cool. Refrigerate for at least 2 hours. Cut into 8 servings.

HINTS: 1. Egg whites beat best at room temperature.

2. Meringue pie cuts easily if you dip a sharp knife in warm water before slicing.

Each serving equals:

HE: ½ Bread • ¼ Protein • ¾ Slider •
15 Optional Calories

159 Calories • 7 gm Fat • 4 gm Protein •
20 gm Carbohydrate • 356 mg Sodium • 0 gm Fiber

DIABETIC: 1 Starch • 1 Fat

Caramel Apple Cheesecake

We never seem to forget the flavors we loved in childhood—maybe because we remember those days with such happiness. This recipe will send your guests on a "flavor flashback" to those sweet and chewy treats we loved so dearly! ❂ Serves 8

1 (8-ounce) package Philadelphia fat-free cream cheese

1 (4-serving) package JELL-O sugar-free instant butterscotch pudding mix

⅔ cup Carnation Nonfat Dry Milk Powder

2 cups unsweetened apple juice☆

¼ cup Cool Whip Lite

1 (6-ounce) Keebler graham cracker piecrust

1 (4-serving) package JELL-O sugar-free vanilla cook-and-serve pudding mix

2 tablespoons Brown Sugar Twin

2 cups (4 small) cored, peeled, and chopped cooking apples

2 tablespoons (½ ounce) chopped pecans

1 teaspoon vanilla extract

In a large bowl, stir cream cheese with a spoon until soft. Add dry instant pudding mix, dry milk powder, and 1 cup apple juice. Mix well using a wire whisk. Blend in Cool Whip Lite. Spread mixture evenly into piecrust. Refrigerate. Meanwhile, in a medium saucepan, combine remaining 1 cup apple juice, dry cook-and-serve pudding mix, and Brown Sugar Twin. Add apples. Mix well to combine. Cook over medium heat, stirring often, until mixture thickens and apples soften slightly. Remove from heat. Stir in pecans and vanilla extract. Place saucepan on a wire rack and allow to cool completely. Spoon cooled apple mixture evenly over cream cheese filling. Refrigerate for at least 1 hour. Cut into 8 servings.

HINT: Good topped with 1 tablespoon Cool Whip Lite, but don't forget to count the few additional calories.

Each serving equals:

HE: 1 Fruit • ½ Bread • ½ Protein • ¼ Fat •

¼ Skim Milk • ¾ Slider • 19 Optional Calories

---

222 Calories • 6 gm Fat • 7 gm Protein •

35 gm Carbohydrate • 565 mg Sodium • 1 gm Fiber

DIABETIC: 1 Starch • 1 Fruit • 1 Fat • ½ Meat *or*

2 Carbohydrate • 1 Fat • ½ Meat

Cherry Celebration Cheesecake ❄

You'll notice that I believe in packing my desserts with abundant flavor, often "doubling up" as I do in this cherry concoction. The combination of the sweet cherries with the cherry gelatin is a culinary home run, quickly bringing the fans to their feet (once they taste it)! Try doubling your pleasure with this one.

❍ Serves 8

> 2 (8-ounce) packages Philadelphia fat-free cream cheese
> 1 (4-serving) package JELL-O sugar-free instant vanilla pudding mix
> 1 (4-serving) package JELL-O sugar-free cherry gelatin
> ⅔ cup Carnation Nonfat Dry Milk Powder
> ¼ cup water
> 1 cup (one 8-ounce can) crushed pineapple, packed in fruit juice, undrained
> ¾ cup Cool Whip Lite☆
> 2 cups (12 ounces) frozen unsweetened pitted bing or sweet cherries, thawed, drained, and chopped
> 1 (6-ounce) Keebler graham cracker piecrust

In a large bowl, stir cream cheese with a spoon until soft. Add dry pudding mix, dry gelatin, dry milk powder, water, and undrained pineapple. Mix well using a wire whisk. Blend in ¼ cup Cool Whip Lite and cherries. Evenly spread mixture into piecrust. Refrigerate for at least 1 hour. Cut into 8 servings. When serving, top each piece with 1 tablespoon Cool Whip Lite.

HINT: Canned sweet cherries, rinsed and drained, or fresh pitted bing cherries may be used in place of frozen.

Each serving equals:

HE: 1 Protein • ¾ Fruit • ½ Bread • ¼ Skim Milk •
1 Slider • 3 Optional Calories

242 Calories • 6 gm Fat • 12 gm Protein •
35 gm Carbohydrate • 698 mg Sodium • 1 gm Fiber

DIABETIC: 1½ Starch • 1 Meat • 1 Fruit • ½ Fat

Index of Recipes

A

Acapulco Tuna Salad, 116
Aloha Dream Pie, 174
Amoré Ham and Cheese Pie, 146
Apple Chocolate Chip Snack Cake, 163
Apple Dessert Bars, 166
Apple Orchard Muffins, 68
Applesauce Pork Balls, 130
Applesauce Spice Cake, 162
Apricot Salad, 93

B

Baked Chicken with Cream Sauce, 119
Baked Ham with Island Sauce, 147
Baked Pork in Cider Gravy, 132
Banana Pecan Bread, 72
Blue Cheese Mushroom Salad, 89
Broccoli and Rice Side Dish, 104
Broccoli-Corn Dish, 102
Buffet Baked Ham Salad, 142
Buffet Egg Casserole, 114

C

Caramel Apple Cheesecake, 180
Carrot Cake Muffins, 66
Carrot-Pineapple Toss, 91
Catalina Isle Salad, 83
Cherry Banana Cream Pie, 172
Cherry Celebration Cheesecake, 182
Cherry Cloud in the Sky Pie, 171
Cherry Waldorf Salad, 92
Chicken-Apple Salad Stuffed Pitas, 120
Chicken Breast Cacciatore with Spaghetti, 124
Chinese Chicken Soup, 63
Chocolate Caribbean Fruit Dip, 59
Chocolate Graham Treats, 151
Chop Suey Pasta Hot Dish, 136
Cinnamon-Apple Corn Bread, 71
Cinnamon Cream Rolls, 70
Coconut Lemon Meringue Pie, 178
Colorful Cauliflower Buffet Salad, 90

Company Fillets, 118
Cordon Bleu Rice Dish, 128
Creamy Fruit-Pecan Salad, 97
Creamy Peas and Corn, 101
Crunchy Munchy Banana Party
    Pie, 170

D
Dill Pickle–Cheese Salad Toss,
    87
Dill Pickle Rings, 60

E
Easy Creamed Green Beans, 99

F
Fall Harvest Fruit Salad, 95
Farmstead Corn Pudding, 106
Festive Ham Salad Buns, 141
Fiesta Cherry Burritos, 156
Frankfurter Spanish Rice, 139
French Copper Pennies, 88
Fresh Strawberry Punch, 73
Frosted Cauliflower/Broccoli
    Bake, 103
Frozen Lemon Yogurt Pie, 168
Fruit Melba Meringue Cups,
    152

G
Garden Cucumber Potato
    Salad, 109
Gazpacho Salad, 82
Grande Bean and Carrot Toss,
    84
Grande Mexican Lasagna, 138
Grande Stuffed Baked Toma-
    toes, 133

H
Ham and Cheese Pinwheels, 62
Ham and Eggs Pizza, 113
Ham and Pea Salad Stuffed To-
    matoes, 74
Harvest Dressing and Turkey,
    126
Hawaiian Apple Salad, 100
Hawaiian Baked Pork Tenders,
    131
Hawaiian Ham Sandwiches,
    143
Hawaiian Mint Dip, 58
He-Man Open-Faced Hoagies,
    134

I
Italian Beef and Noodle Soup,
    65
Italian Ham Rotini, 145

L
Lemon Blueberry Cream Pie,
    175
Lime Chiffon Banana Pie, 169

M
Macaroni and Tuna Salad, 117
Mexican Potato Salad, 108
Mixed Fruit Salad, 96
Molded Garden Salad, 81
Mustard Cucumber Salad, 85

P
Party Pizza Bites, 77
Party-Time Baked Beans, 107
Party-Time Chicken Salad, 122
Pasta with Carrots and Ham,
    144

Peachy Keen Salad, 94
Peanut Butter Candy Drops,
    150
Pineapple Pecan Pudding
    Shortcake, 158
Pistachio Delight, 154
Pumpkin-Pecan Crunch, 160

R
Rainbow Tossed Salad, 86
Raisin Pecan Meringue Pie,
    176
Raspberry Almond Cream Pie,
    173
Rhubarb Custard Pizza, 164
Rio Taco Pie, 140

S
Salad Bar Pizza, 76
Salsa Party Dip, 58
Sauerkraut Pizza, 135
Scalloped Carrots and Celery,
    98
Skillet Hamburger Celery Stro-
    ganoff, 137
Swiss Tomato-Corn Bake, 105

T
Thai Pork Soup, 64
Tuna Garden Wedges, 75

V
Veggie Salad Rye Rounds, 61

:0

I want to hear from you...

Besides my family, the love of my life is creating "common folk" healthy recipes and solving everyday cooking questions in *The Healthy Exchanges Way*. Everyone who uses my recipes is considered part of the Healthy Exchanges Family, so please write to me if you have any questions, comments, or suggestions. I will do my best to answer. With your support, I'll continue to stir up even more recipes and cooking tips for the Family in the years to come.

Write to: JoAnna M. Lund
c/o Healthy Exchanges, Inc.
P.O. Box 124
DeWitt, IA 52742

If you prefer, you can call me at 1-319-659-8234, fax me at 1-319-659-2126, or contact me via E-mail by writing to HealthyJo @aol.com.

Now that you've seen Party Fare, why not order The Healthy Exchanges Food Newsletter?

If you enjoyed the recipes in this cookbook and would like to cook up even more of these "common folk" healthy dishes, you may want to subscribe to *The Healthy Exchanges Food Newsletter*.

This monthly 12-page newsletter contains 30-plus new recipes *every month* in such columns as:

- Reader Exchange
- Reader Requests
- Recipe Makeover
- Micro Corner
- Dinner for Two

- Crock Pot Luck
- Meatless Main Dishes
- Rise & Shine
- Our Small World

- Brown Bagging It
- Snack Attack
- Side Dishes
- Main Dishes
- Desserts

In addition to all the recipes, other regular features include:
- The Editor's Motivational Corner
- Dining Out Question & Answer
- Cooking Question & Answer
- New Product Alert
- Success Profiles of Winners in the Losing Game
- Exercise Advice from a Cardiac Rehab Specialist
- Nutrition Advice from a Registered Dietitian
- Positive Thought for the Month

Just as in this cookbook, all *Healthy Exchanges Food Newsletter* recipes are calculated in three distinct ways: 1) Weight Loss Choices, 2) Calories with Fat and Fiber Grams, and 3) Diabetic Exchanges.

The cost for a one-year (12-issue) subscription with a special Healthy Exchanges 3-ring binder to store the newsletters in is $27.50. To order, simply complete the form and mail to us *or* call our toll-free number and pay with your VISA or MasterCard.

_____ Yes, I want to subscribe to *The Healthy Exchanges Food Newsletter.* $27.50 Yearly Subscription Cost .... $_____

_____ Foreign orders please add $6.00 for money exchange and extra postage .... $_____

_____ I'm not sure, so please send me a sample copy at $2.50 .... $_____

Please make check payable to HEALTHY EXCHANGES or pay by VISA/MasterCard

CARD NUMBER:_____ EXPIRATION DATE:_____

SIGNATURE:_____

Signature required for all credit card orders.

Or order toll-free, using your credit card, at 1-800-766-8961

NAME: _____

ADDRESS: _____

CITY _____ STATE _____ ZIP _____

TELEPHONE: ( ) _____

If additional orders for the newsletter are to be sent to an address other than the one listed above, please use a separate sheet and attach to this form.

MAIL TO: **HEALTHY EXCHANGES**
P.O. BOX 124
DeWitt, IA 52742-0124

1-800-766-8961 For Customer Orders
1-319-659-8234 For Customer Service

Thank you for your order, and for choosing to become a part of the Healthy Exchanges Family!

About the Author

JoAnna M. Lund is the author of *Healthy Exchanges Cookbook; HELP: Healthy Exchanges Lifetime Plan;* and *The Diabetic's Healthy Exchanges Cookbook.* She has been profiled in national and local publications, including *People, The New York Times, Forbes,* and *The National Enquirer,* and has appeared on hundreds of radio and television shows. A popular speaker with weight loss, cardiac, and diabetic support groups, she can be seen weekly on public television with her show *Help Yourself with JoAnna Lund.*